Standing on His Shoulders

Standing on His Shoulders

What I Learned about Race, Life, and High
Expectations from My Haitian Superman Father

DAVID J MALEBRANCHE

ISBN: 0996456600
ISBN 13: 9780996456609
Library of Congress Control Number: 2015908751
3dotpress, Philadelphia, PA

This book is dedicated to my mother, Donna Marie Shinglar Malebranche – the strength, heart and soul of our family, and the wind beneath my wings for as long as I can remember.

I celebrate every Black man in America. We are all sons, fathers, or both during our lifetimes. We must learn to love, understand, and appreciate each other and ourselves to improve our social, physical, and emotional health worldwide.

Acknowledgements

Thanks to Boyd Baker, for your careful content and copy editing of this manuscript, feedback, and insightful suggestions as a reader and father. Harley Etienne, for being a great friend, supporter, and introducing me to Boyd when I was searching for a copy editor. Derick Wilson, for encouraging me to purchase the text that helped me move this project forward. Anthony Roberts Jr., for your professional wisdom and Millennial sage advice. Taylor Goodell Benedum for your graphic design wizardry and patience with me. Finally, to John Peterson for being the best mentor, uncle, and friend I could've asked for, and your invaluable early review of this manuscript.

I have been blessed to have many family and friends support me in my journey thus far. Thanks to everyone who has helped me and been in my corner along the way, especially the mentors who guided me, and the mentees who trusted in me enough to allow me to guide them.

Table of Contents

Preface

My father is undoubtedly the Superman I always thought he was. As a child, this statement was more superficial, as I truly believed he was all-powerful, all-knowing, and had no faults. He was well-informed, could do and fix anything, and would always be there to save the day. Fortunately for both of us, as we have grown older and our relationship has gone through various ups and downs, I realized Dad is a different kind of Superman - a living, breathing human being who, despite being a strong man, is not impenetrable and cannot leap tall buildings in a single bound. He doesn't always do or say the right thing, has his own set of personal insecurities, and hasn't always been able to be there when I needed him most. While some may view this realization as a disappointment, for me it has only made me appreciate him that much more.

Dad is my hero because it is hard to bring a child into this world and raise that child in the United States, particularly a young Black man. It is a complex task to instruct that child on how to navigate general society's perceptions of what it means to be a man. It is quite a challenge to raise a young boy to do this while journeying through a society that doesn't affirm Black life, actively promotes racial profiling, continues targeted "stop and frisk" policies, and has a pre-conceived notion that you are going to fail simply because of the color of your skin. There are no books, manuals, directions, or "How To" guides providing proper instructions on how to be a good father to a son growing up with these intersecting life pressures. When Dad came to the United States from Haiti in the early1960s, he didn't get the memo that having low expectations of Black men was the norm in this country. He didn't grasp the concept of a constructed social hierarchy based on race and ethnicity. He didn't realize that Black men were and continue to be seen as target practice for some prejudiced police officers. He simply came here to explore opportunities and, after starting a family, be a good provider. Many men jump at the opportunity to create a child, but fold under the responsibility of guiding that child to become a well-functioning adult. Although some of my friends would happily point out my dysfunctional qualities, the fact that I can sit to write this book is a testament to how amazing my father truly is. Dad had a plan for his children. He and my mother chose to support us through our journeys. And for that I am truly thankful.

Dad wasn't about embracing the absentee father experience that is pawned off as the norm in Black communities today. Ever since I was young, I have always heard the incessant media reports about how Black fathers are an endangered species, often geographically, emotionally, physically, or psychologically absent in our lives. Unfortunately, some may have even abused us at times in various physical, mental, sexual, or psychological ways. Many Black men proudly proclaim they have "made it" *despite* not having a biological father present while growing up. There are Father's Day cards specifically targeting single Black mothers, acknowledging them for assuming many traditionally paternal roles when raising their children. Even President Barack Obama's memoir *Dreams from my Father: A Story of Race and Inheritance* tells of how he succeeded in spite of not having his Kenyan father around growing up. While these stories exist and are the reality for many Black men, they are not exclusive to Black communities, nor are they the only narratives of Black fathers that exist. There are droves of Black fathers who stand tall, are present every day, and serve as consistent positive influences in our lives. Every day these men breathe, work, and exist to support their children, undeterred by whether the mainstream media recognizes them or not.

My relationship with my father has been an odyssey through passageways where there is a lesson to be learned around every corner. He is partly responsible for my entry into this world. He gave me the primary example of what it means to be a man, even when the extent of my physical interactions with him was minimal or turbulent. When I thought about it, I owed it to him and myself to reconsider how our relationship has shaped me into the man I am today. Instead of simply asking, "Why did he act like that?" or "Where was he that time when I needed him?" I was challenged to instead ask, "What did he experience in his life before I was born?" and "What am I supposed to learn from his life that I can apply to my own?" The answers I found by asking these latter questions not only addressed my narrow perceptions of good or bad parenting – but also shed light on behaviors that I was having trouble understanding. I started to appreciate the context from which Dad emerged, and this was invaluable in developing a more positive relationship with him. The process of re-learning my Dad has helped me realize not only the heroic and flawed qualities he possesses, but my own as well.

I originally set out to write this book as a personal form of therapy. For years I was confused and struggled to understand my father, his motivations, and his perspective. I couldn't see him for the nuanced man he was back then, but viewed him through the tainted lens of my childhood experiences that I carried with me through adulthood like unwanted baggage. There are many life lessons he taught me and I wanted to thank him. I was also tortured by a lack of forgiveness in my heart for how I didn't experience him as present while I was growing up. I clung to an archaic notion that being present as a father solely referred to a physical presence – being in the same house, in the same room, engaged in an activity together. If Dad wasn't fulfilling these criteria, he was not being a good father. In essence, if he was not living up to the perfectionist standards set by TV dads like Bill Cosby's Cliff Huxtable, he was falling short of his paternal responsibilities.

As I continued writing and reflecting on my relationship with him, I came to understand that I was remembering him wrong. I needed to get it right.

As I began to construct these chapters detailing my experiences with Dad, I also started hearing similar narratives when discussing the issue of fathers among my friends and colleagues. While I was engaged in doing focus groups and interviews as part of my public health research involving sexual health among Black men, the topic of father-son relationships inevitably came up. No matter the context or question, when we started to discuss childhood experiences in the lives of Black men, the profound importance of how we remembered our relationships with our fathers always emerged. The exact experiences weren't the same – but the notion of how crucial these relationships were in forming our adult selves could not be denied. I also learned that many Black men, like me, had personally experienced an alternative and affirming counternarrative to the absentee Black father accounts that dominate today's news reports. We must sing these stories from the highest mountaintop.

Standing on his Shoulders is a story about my Dad and me. It is a tale of how I have experienced him over the course of my life – from wide-eyed wonderment to disappointment, then forgiveness, understanding, and ultimately profound appreciation. While some of the lessons I will describe may resonate with fathers and sons of all races and ethnicities, this story is specifically about a Black father born in Haiti and his son born in America. To dilute or deny that race and racism hasn't played a role in both of our lived experiences would be dishonest to ourselves, and would dishonor our ancestors who came before us.

To tell this story properly, I couldn't simply start with my birth. I had to start by detailing the origins of both my parents. The first three chapters offer a brief retelling of their lives before they met, and the beginning of their journey together before my sister Michelle and I were born. During Thanksgiving weekend 2012, I sat down with both my mother and father individually so they could tell me, in their own words, about their lives growing up and how they met. They were both remarkably candid when discussing their childhoods. Each one cried at times, recalling the people who meant the most to them in their lives, particularly when describing challenging moments in their histories. Their formative experiences were extraordinarily similar despite coming from different countries and contrasting racial backgrounds. In many ways, it's not surprising at all that their paths crossed when they did.

What I truly enjoyed when listening to my parents tell their stories was hearing about *how they became who they are.* We all think we truly know our parents and can construct a decent recollection of them from memory alone. This is a fallacy. When you sit across from the individuals who brought you into this world and listen with nothing but an audio recorder bearing witness, their stories blossom into life - the triumphs, the tragedies, the disappointments, and every important milestone. All of it becomes a living, breathing testimony, steeped in oral history and tradition. After you hear these stories, you will never see your parents the same way again. For anyone who thinks they know the entirety of their parents' history, sit with them and ask them to tell it to you. Let them take their time while you embrace the role of being nothing but a good listener. You'll soon realize how much you thought you knew, but had no idea.

Whether or not your biological father was physically present in your life as you grew up - this book is for you. Whether he took a personal investment in your future or at times didn't seem interested at all – this book is for you. Whether he could give you all the material possessions you needed or couldn't give you anything but the love in his heart – this book is for you. Whether you love him unconditionally or harbor resentment towards him – this book is for you. Regardless of how our relationships with our biological fathers have existed and flowed over the years, the fact remains that this one man has the most profound impact on our lives as men, whether we want to admit it or not. The lessons we learn about ourselves from our relationships with our fathers are what make us the men we eventually become. *Standing on his Shoulders* is the story of one such relationship, from a proud son's perspective. I am not here in spite of him. I am here because of him.

I

MESSIAH

My father's life, in his own words, was complex. Roger Joseph Malebranche was born in the small Haitian town of Anse-à-Veau in 1932, the son of Adrien Malebranche and Celanie Beaudin. The Haiti that raised him is a far cry from the one whose common description only highlights abject poverty, overpopulation, government corruption, and the scourge of HIV. The Haiti my father knew had almost 3 million inhabitants and shared the island known as Hispanola with the Dominican Republic. Anse-à-Veau, which loosely translates into "Bay of Cattle" in English, was a gorgeous coastal town of about 2000 people, boasting land rich in natural goods, spices, coffee, and other resources. There was an uptown and a downtown that was merely geographic and not based on financial or economic status. Adrien Malebranche, better known as "Papa," was a dynamic young man whose demeanor dripped swagger like melted ice cream off a sugar cone. He was six feet tall with a wiry strong build, rich mahogany skin, and a booming laugh that matched his ebullient and playful spirit. Papa's family lived on the seashore in the downtown area with all its rustic and majestic beauty - a perfect location for a kidnapping.

Dad's first memory was the crackling of dry tree leaves under Papa's calloused feet. Papa had come to Anse-à-Veau to ask Celanie if he could take young Roger for a visit to his mother Grand Dede and sister Tante Jeanne in Port-au-Prince. Celanie said yes, not knowing that his plan was to never bring him back. Papa didn't get along with Celanie's father, and her brothers didn't much care for him either. He was the type of man every respectable family would tell their daughters to avoid. Papa owned a rickety car while working in northern Haiti, which only took him so far on the island's unpaved and treacherous roads. At one point during the journey, he was forced to leave his car, scoop his young son in his arms, and hurry by foot up the steep slopes of Morne L'Hopital, the picturesque mountains overlooking Port-au-Prince. He dropped Dad off with Gran Dede and Tante Jeanne, and disappeared in the northern part of the country. Celanie was devastated, and despite the family searching the countryside high and low for her son, they couldn't find him. She returned to Anse-à-Veau brokenhearted that her first born child had been taken away from her. Dad wouldn't see his biological mother again until he was six years old.

Dad's next memory was sitting on Tante Jeanne's knees in Morne L'Hopital, gazing through the rain on the panorama of Port-au-Prince and its bay 4000 feet below. Morne

L'Hopital was a glorious setting, with flowers everywhere, and lush vibrant foliage waiting to greet him in every direction. This was a breathtakingly beautiful Haiti, the country that sweetly caressed him in her affirming arms and let him know how special he truly was. The first independent Black republic insisted on reminding him of his abundant worth and intelligence, and that he could be anything he wanted to be. He would be raised by Gran Dede and Tante Jeanne during these formative years. Tante Jeanne, despite being his biological aunt, essentially became his mother.

Tante Jeanne was undoubtedly the biggest influence in Dad's life, and someone he regrets me never meeting in person. A cocoa-colored woman with high cheekbones and piercing eyes, she could be loving and stern at the same time without the slightest whiff of contradiction. Tante Jeanne was an educator and the first female teacher at the biggest school in Haiti, an all-male Catholic school named Institute de Saint Louis de Gonzague. She would eventually become the principal tutor for the young Baby Doc Duvalier, before he became Haiti's president from 1971 to 1986. As a mother, Tante Jeanne was the most intelligent person Dad ever knew, and she had a very complicated relationship with Papa. She never refrained from expressing her feelings that her brother was not worthy of being Dad's father. Papa was a charmer, a ladies' man, and someone who comfortably nestled into the absentee father stereotype. Yet he never shied away from taking credit for Dad's academic success. My father only saw Papa every 2-3 months after he delivered him to Morne L'Hopital. Soon after, Papa remarried and started a whole new family.

Dad's mother Celanie did the same. Thus Dad became the only child of his parents' union but later gained a plethora of half-brothers and sisters. He didn't fully reconnect with Papa until he was around 14, when Tante Jeanne left the mountain and brought him to Port-au-Prince where she had accepted a teaching position.

The Institute de Saint Louis de Gonzague was a Roman Catholic primary and secondary school located in downtown Port-au-Prince, and the place where Dad sharpened his intellectual acuity as a child. The Haitian elite and French dignitaries sent all their best and brightest children there. They were the sons and daughters of rich merchants, diplomats, and powerful politicians, all instructed by a core of Irish, French, Haitian, and French-Canadian teachers. A beautiful, gothic church sat adjacent to the school, and all the young Haitian students attended every Sunday morning in their standard uniforms: cap with SLG insignia, double-breasted blazer, and white pressed and creased pants. They even had a choir and a football team. Many years after Dad completed his studies there, Tante Jeanne became the first lay person and first Black secular woman asked by the priests to join their teaching staff.

In the old French system, Haitian children went from kindergarten through Rhetoric and Philosophy. Those two phases of schooling include what in the American system would be grade school, high school, and college. After both phases are completed, students took a two-part national Baccalaureat exam. With successful completion, they could then attend grad school. The families who were well established in Haiti all had access to this higher level of educational training according to their grades and intellectual capabilities. When Francois "Papa Doc" Duvalier came into power in 1957 however, all of that changed. Papa Doc wanted to equalize all the social classes and abolished any kind of academic standards when it came to the quality of the children admitted to these schools. This was particularly evident with the admission into graduate law and medical programs, which ultimately led to the erosion of the traditional schooling system in Haiti. As a result of these policies, many of the most talented Haitians left the island for the perceived greener pastures of Europe, Africa, and the United States. Haiti was essentially robbed of some of its sharpest minds, and Dad became one of many who joined the exodus.

Dad attended medical school at L'Université d'Etat d'Haiti, which required a first year of physics, chemistry, and biology, called "PCB." Four more years of classes were followed by one year of training in a hospital, after which he had to pass a final exam to graduate. He was at the top of his class and had his choice of where he could go to complete his medical residency training after graduation, so he took a position as a physician at the seashore town of Port-à-Piment du Sud. The territory he covered stretched across the coast of southern Haiti from Les Anglais to Port Salut. Dad had a jeep, a horse, and a mule with which to cover six seashore towns. He traveled across the pristine beaches overlooking the ocean, providing medical care to people suffering from tuberculosis, malaria, typhoid fever, cholera, and other chronic illnesses. He often describes this period as the best time of his life – he felt like he was necessary, doing something that mattered, and putting his God-given talents to good use. It was 1957, Dad was only twenty-five years old, a newly minted physician in his home country. The girls were pretty, the work was challenging, and he was healing individuals who really needed his help. What was there not to like?

After completing his medical service in Port-à-Piment du Sud, Dad could practice wherever he desired. Most young Haitian physicians ventured to Europe or Canada for employment opportunities, not the United States. He had secured a fellowship in Paris in Internal Medicine, but before he was about to leave, there was the matter of completing a medical clearance physical. He was honest and admitted to the doctor his history of contracting malaria two months prior. The physician told him he would have to take medications to treat it and they were required to keep him quarantined until three separate blood tests proved he was clear of the infection.

Dad still could have accepted the Paris fellowship after he finished his treatment, but the pharmaceutical company Eli Lily chose him as the young physician who would receive their medical fellowship in New York at Columbia University. Jacques Prosper, a close friend and fellow physician who had just moved from Haiti to Harlem for an American internship, encouraged Dad to come to the United States. At first he wasn't too keen on the idea. He knew that America was a very racist country, and the prospect of placing himself in that kind of environment after growing up in Haiti was not that appealing. Jacques was persuasive in his marketing of the American dream to my father however, so Dad decided to accept Eli Lily's offer. He figured he could do the fellowship in New York for one year and return to Haiti in 1962.

The climate in Haiti was changing as my father prepared to embark on his journey to the United States. Political instability was becoming the norm, and Papa Doc Duvalier was killing more and more intellectuals every day. Tante Jeanne advised him to stay in the U.S once he landed there safely. He had been offered additional medical training at Ellis Hospital in Schenectady, New York – a prospect Tante Jeanne thought would make her son a more well-rounded doctor upon his return to Haiti. All of Dad's family and friends supported that decision, and the money he made in the U.S. was OK, so he stayed. Most importantly, Tante Jeanne supported his continuing education in the United States, and that meant the world to him. Papa had gotten into trouble with members of the Tonton Macoute militia in Haiti and fled to the U.S. because he feared for his life. A rich, American friend in upstate New York hired him to work as a chauffeur. This reunited Dad and Papa in a small way, though they still did not see much of each other.

Tante Jeanne used to write Dad long letters on a weekly basis while he served as Chief Resident of Surgery at Ellis Hospital. She always began each letter by calling him "Toutou," a commonly used French term of endearment. Papa Doc Duvalier had hired her to be the private tutor for his son Jean-Claude, "Baby Doc," and her role as his instructor was expanding exponentially. No less than three times a week, a chauffeured limousine would pick her up and drive her to the Presidential Palace so she could tutor the future president. Her letters were a lifeline to Dad, keeping him connected to Haiti and his beloved mother. One weekend, however, after returning from a surgical conference in New York City, a telegram arrived from Haiti saying that Tante Jeanne was sick and he should return home immediately. He knew it was serious, but wasn't allowed to travel because he had an exchange visa which required him to get a travel permit before he could leave the U.S. The ominous message was delivered on a Saturday but he couldn't depart until Wednesday. By the time he landed in Port-au-Prince, Tante Jeanne had already died from complications of a cerebral hemorrhage and had been buried.

When Dad speaks of Tante Jeanne's premature passing, his eyes become glassy and heavy with loss. He regrets never getting the chance to say a proper goodbye to the inventive woman who was the most important influence in his life. She would've given the world to him if she could have, and not seeing her before she died is something he often says he will take with him to his grave. Tante Jeanne educated countless local children in Port-au-Prince, and taught him everything he knew from the age of two until he was a young man. He wouldn't have stayed in the United States if she had lived. She was only 48 years old and left this earth way too soon. Her passing changed the trajectory of his journey, but afforded him the opportunity to meet another phenomenal woman who would lift his spirit out of mourning.

2

CINDERELLA

Hard work has always been a familiar concept to my mother. Donna Marie Shinglar was born in 1946, the daughter of Basil Shinglar and Mary Basher, and the granddaughter of Ukrainian immigrants. She was raised in the sleepy upstate New York town of Granville, situated in the northeast part of the state near Glens Falls. Due to the multicolored slate that their mines quarried, Granville was affectionately known as the "Colored Slate Capitol of the World." Despite this broad slate diversity, 99% of the town's 2000 inhabitants were White. Her father owned and managed a local bar in town, the maintenance of which occupied the majority of his time during Mom's childhood. Her mother was a stay-at-home mom who took care of her and her brother Bill.

Granville was a stone's throw from being a one horse country town back then, complete with a Main Street, a well-known family physician, and only one Black family. The White people in Granville, while financially modest in means, were abundantly rich with diverse European ancestry. They boasted Irish, Slavic, and Italian origins, each occupying distinct sections in town. Racial diversity, however, was nowhere to be found, and intolerance for other races seemed to be a genetic predisposition for many of Granville's inhabitants. Mom's family, on more than one occasion, instructed her as a child to cross to the other side of the street if she saw a member of the Black family walking towards her on the sidewalk. That was just the way it was.

Mom was only seven years old when her mother Mary first fell ill. She had a mysterious illness that no one in the family discussed, though it took permanent residence in their lives like an unwelcome squatter. It was likely some form of stomach, uterine, or ovarian cancer that forced Mary to spend an excessive amount of time in Albany Medical Center undergoing multiple surgeries and invasive procedures. Before disease smothered Mary in its suffocating arms, Mom had enjoyed a special relationship with her. She was the kind of mother who would do special things for her daughter. She would make a poached egg for her every morning instead of the less expensive pancakes, because she knew that her daughter didn't like pancakes. During the cold winter months she would place Mom's shoes in the oven to warm them up before she sent her out to brave the chilly one-mile walk to school. She glided with a peace and tranquility that starkly contrasted with the bullish nature of a racially-intolerant father who spent the majority of his time working in his bar.

When Mary got sick in 1953 and started going in and out of the hospital, she lost a great deal of weight. She came home the first time with a sturdy hospital bed designed to make her more comfortable than her regular bed. Home care nurses visited her on occasion to help with daily activities, but she never fully regained her health long enough to resume her duties as a mother. Mom came home from school one day to find all the doors locked, and their house as silent as a graveyard. She waited on the porch for hours until one of the neighbors came over and told her that her mother was in the hospital again. Mary's stints in and out of the hospital became a routine part of Mom's childhood, and the loneliness she felt as a result sat with her on most days like a familiar friend. The times when Mary was out of the hospital and home were not joyous ones - she could barely keep down a morsel of food and was unable to keep up with even the most rudimentary activities of daily living. Despite knowing this, the rest of the family would often gather and eat a full meal in front of her as if she wasn't there. Mary never complained, not about the horrific pain she endured or the agony of her family's indifference to her suffering. She wasn't the type of person to hold a grudge or complain - but Mom was paying attention the whole time.

Since her mother was sick and her father spent most of his time at his bar, Mom ended up staying with her Aunt Pauline and Uncle Bob, who had no children of their own. Aunt Pauline caught tuberculosis not long after Mom moved in, and had to be admitted to a local sanitarium for intensive antibiotic treatment. The family then sent her to live with her Ukrainian immigrant grandmother and grandfather who spoke no English. Many times they sent Mom to the local grocery store with instructions and lists of items in Slavic, only to get upset because she would always return with the wrong groceries. Mom's tenure living with them didn't last long. Next she was sent to stay with her Uncle John, who, like her father, exhibited an uncanny intolerance of racial diversity. Uncle John and his wife Terri had three kids of their own, but watched over Mom during those difficult years when her mother was sick and going in and out of various hospitals. Mary Basher's fight for survival ended in 1956 when she was forty-two. Mom was only nine at the time when her mother transitioned. Her brother Bill was four. It was hard for Mom to discern which was more traumatic – watching her mother slowly deteriorate from a robust woman to skin on bones, or the inability to truly call anyplace home.

Mom was old enough to comprehend her mother's death and what that meant. Everything normal before her passing was now strange and chaotic. Her father couldn't run a business and take care of his kids at the same time, so he asked his sister, Aunt Tessie, to take care of her and Bill. At first, Aunt Tessie said no, but later agreed to only take Bill in, not Mom. Aunt Tessie never explained why she refused to take Mom in with Bill after their mother died, but that snub still haunts her to this day. To make matters worse, Uncle John then decided that he couldn't take care of her anymore. He and Aunt Terri were having marital problems. They were fighting a lot and compounding the misery Mom was already experiencing. So after her mother's death, the family had a big meeting at her grandmother's house to discuss who "had" to take care of her while she sat in the room and listened. Mom was nine years old and had just lost her mother after a prolonged two-year illness that they all witnessed firsthand. Yet no one in the family was willing to take her in. Ultimately, her father's sister, Aunt Mary and her husband George said they would take Mom in and look after her.

Aunt Mary and Uncle George had one biological son of their own, Philip. Philip was mean and about two or three years younger than Mom, and used to tease her mercilessly. He resented her presence in their home and how it disrupted the family dynamics he was used to as an only child. The years she stayed with them were challenging. Aunt Mary taught her how to do many chores around the house and was also the first family member to take the time to teach her how to cook. Yet with each and every learning moment Aunt Mary would impart, there was Philip, poised and prepared to do whatever he could to make her stay there unpleasant.

Philip derived gleeful satisfaction out of untying Mom's apron while she was trying to do dishes. He would slyly reach around to her back, yank the tie and watch it come undone, suspending the completion of her chores. She would then have to stop what she was doing and dry her hands to retie her apron. Philip employed this familiar torture technique over and over again, and Mom tried desperately to ignore him and focus on the task at hand, not wanting to get in any trouble. His taunts became too much as the days and weeks passed on. Given everything that had transpired over her young life, she just couldn't take it anymore. She couldn't take the anguish of losing her mother being bottled inside. She couldn't take the pain of having a father who seemed more interested in his bar than her. She couldn't take the sinking feeling that nothing in her blossoming life would ever be permanent and stable. So when she saw caught Philip in the corner of her eye reaching for her apron tie one more time, her reaction was immediate. Mom leaned back slightly, clenched her tiny fist, and unleashed it with the ferocity of a startled lion. Her knuckles made acquaintance with his obnoxious jaw. Philip recoiled, then retrieved a pair of hot tongs and grasped Mom's hand with them, burning her in the process. This was to be her existence while she served her time in Aunt Mary and Uncle George's house.

Mom rarely saw her father Basil after her mother died, despite him living alone in a trailer near Aunt Mary and Uncle George. His work schedule at the bar made it difficult to spend any quality time together. He lost the bar, due to his own staff stealing from him, only to open another on Main Street after he recouped some of his money. Not long after, he was diagnosed with laryngeal cancer, a byproduct of years of continual smoking. The family took him to Roswell Park Hospital in Buffalo for treatment. The doctors performed vocal cord surgery on him, which damaged his voice so much that he had to learn how to speak again. This was yet another life stressor in a series for Mom, but it afforded her the opportunity to spend more time with her dad because he was now vulnerable and needed her to help him at the bar. Mom cleaned every inch of that bar more times than she could count, and also did other odd jobs to make his life easier. In turn, he taught her a lot about banking, deposits, check balancing, and other skills that come with running a company. She studied him intently, watching how he cashed the checks for the men who worked at the local quarry. He would allow them to deposit their checks with him, and many would promptly spend their hard-earned money at his bar getting drunk. Basil Shinglar made it so his helping them out with their checks was ultimately good for his business.

Mom's residence with Aunt Mary and Uncle George continued, despite Philip's overt objections and interference. Aunt Mary was very strict and a firm disciplinarian. She was the type of person you never asked "why" when she asked you to do something, as the answer always was always a resounding "because I said so." No discussion. No compromise. Uncle George was much easier to get along with. He treated Mom better than any other family member she could remember. He used to take her hunting with him and would show her how to shoot and cut up deer. He became something of a father figure to her while her own father was busy working at the bar.

Mom also had an Aunt Anna on her Dad's side of the family who had a summer camp on Lake St. Catherine. Every spring Aunt Anna invited Mom to join her and her five kids at the lake for two weeks. Aunt Anna's intentions, however, weren't just to have her there to have a good time – she was expected to help clean up the camp for summer use. Aunt Anna's own children weren't tasked to do the same chores Mom was. She made her work to enjoy the courtesy of being allowed to stay there a couple weeks during the year. By that time, Mom was becoming painfully accustomed to this being her role in the family. She just silently put her blinders on, deliberate in doing anything she was asked to keep things peaceful and calm.

In junior high and high school, Mom grew into a bright, young woman. She triumphantly rose from the embers of her mother's death, revolving homes, and daily microaggressions, recognizing that it was now her time to fly. She started branching out and enjoying herself a little more, developing friendships with local kids in the area. She still stayed with Aunt Mary and Uncle George, and started getting involved in cheerleading and other school activities. Mom wasn't a stellar student, but received good enough grades to get her through. The days of trauma, loss, and instability were becoming increasingly distant memories with which she was all too happy to part.

In the early 1960's, young women in Granville had three options for their career paths: secretary, teacher, or nurse. For Mom, the obvious choice was nursing. While visiting her Aunt Anna in Schenectady, she was introduced to being a candy striper, the equivalent of a volunteer female hospital worker. Candy stripers lived in the hospital dorms and were given meals in exchange for performing daily patient care duties that medical assistants get paid to do today. Mom took pride in being a candy striper and taking care of patients, and on weekends she would spend time with Aunt Anna. She was a born nurturer.

Schenectady was also the place where Mom experienced a rude awakening that clashed with her upbringing in Granville.

She was now being exposed to a much more racially and culturally diverse community of people, doctors, and patients. It struck her that everyone got sick and everyone bled the same color blood. So why did her family and so many others in Granville harbor so much animosity for people who weren't White? By the time she entered nursing school at the age of seventeen, Mom fully understood that there was a big world outside of Granville. A world she was ready to embrace with open arms after what seemed like a lifetime of heartache. A new residence she could call home. A city where she would meet the man who would be the perfect fit.

3

Against the World

It was 1965 when my mother first informed my father she wasn't interested in having lunch with him. Racial tension lingered on every street corner and bus stop, the messy afterbirth of slavery and Jim Crow laws. Systematic institutions of White supremacy stood on the proverbial neck of Black people, making it hard for anyone to breathe. Folks were tired, but fighting back – and the war was getting rough. Malcolm X's body was being riddled with bullets and the Watts Riots reduced once-intact neighborhoods to rubble in Los Angeles. Somewhere in Selma, Alabama, a handsome, charismatic, Baptist preacher was leading thousands on street marches and sit-in protests. Despite vigorous opposition, The Voting Rights Act, guaranteeing Black people the right to vote, became law. The United States was in the middle of an intense Civil Rights Movement.

Standing on His Shoulders

In Schenectady, a beautifully resilient young White woman from Granville was about to cross paths with a charming, young Black man hailing from Anse-à-Veau. At Ellis Hospital, Donna Shinglar was training as a nurse while Roger Malebranche was completing his own surgical indoctrination. Schenectady was a working class, predominantly White town, and the home of the large energy and technology conglomerate General Electric. Most of the Black people who lived in Schenectady worked in service jobs. A Black Haitian surgical resident gracing the halls of the city's main hospital was something of a unicorn at that time, so there was quite a spotlight shed on Dad and anything he did. Being raised in a country where Black excellence was the rule, not the exception, he was blithely unaware that his words and actions were being interpreted as reflective of an entire race of people.

The hospital cafeteria culture at Ellis Hospital in the 1960s was nothing short of a *Grey's Anatomy* episode. Virile male medical residents congregated to watch the cattle call of young, voluptuous female nurses and nursing students as they sauntered by. Attending physicians intellectually and psychologically tortured their inexperienced mentees. Dad was completing a clinical fellowship in Boston when Mom arrived at Ellis. His reputation was whispered in her ear long before she met him in person. He was known as a womanizer of sorts, a racialized myth that envisioned White women as chaste and pure and Black men as sexual predators. When she first laid eyes on him, he was huddled up close to a young female nurse in the underground corridor between the nursing school and the hospital. His arms, reaching over the nurse's head and shoulders while touching the wall, appeared to have her pinned. Yet she didn't seem uncomfortable with his close positioning. They were having a conversation, possibly frivolous or innocent banter, and the body language was close, familiar. The type of interaction suggesting a deeper intimacy that made the Granville native say to herself, "that must be Dr. Malebranche."

Dad first saw Mom in the Ellis Hospital library where she was studying. He was unfamiliar with this beautiful, young woman from Granville, New York with haunting hazel eyes. She was small framed with a demure countenance: a portrait of composure and elegance. How did he not know her? And more importantly, why hadn't she spoken to him yet? Here he was, Chief Resident of Surgery at Ellis Hospital, accustomed to operating room doctors, nurses, and staff giving him all the attention he needed and then some. Yet this young Miss Shinglar was aloof, distant, and apparently unconcerned with his existence. These perplexing, unanswered questions prompted him to ask another nursing student about her – did she have something against Blacks? Was she racist? The nursing student friend of Mom's informed her that Dr. Malebranche was asking if she was racist, a question to which she replied, "He doesn't need other women." Mom didn't want to be another casualty in the wake of the man affectionately known as the "Messiah of the Operating Room."

The bruised ego of a proud Haitian man is hard to contain, so he decided to approach her. Dad sat directly across from her at the library table and unleashed the full arsenal of his suave accent and Caribbean charm.

"Miss Shinglar, were you planning on getting something to eat?" he asked.

"Yes," she replied, her gaze steadily fixed on the textbook in front of her.

"Would you like to go get something to eat with me?" he continued.

"No," she responded bluntly. She felt uncomfortable at that moment, so she simply got up and left. That was their first interaction.

He asked her out to dinner and lunch several times after that, strategically positioning himself across from her at the same table, in the same library, only to become further acquainted with the same rejection. A few weeks later, Mom did accept a dinner date offer, but not from Dad. Instead, a young Indian surgical resident who also worked at Ellis Hospital got the opportunity to take her out. This colleague was a man the Haitian Messiah considered one of his subordinates but a good person nonetheless. Upon hearing the news that this other doctor and Miss Shinglar went out on a date after she had rejected him multiple times, he made it his life's mission to keep asking her out until she gave in. The resilient 2nd generation Ukrainian put up a good fight, but eventually his Haitian persistence broke her down, and she acquiesced. They would have dinner together.

Dad didn't think anything of Mom being White and what that potentially meant in the racial climate of the day. To him, she was just another member of the human race. He had trained at Columbia University in Manhattan in 1961, and had lived in the International House at that time. Racial and ethnic diversity in the female species was a concept with which he was quite familiar. He had tried dating many Black American women before, and many wouldn't give him the time of day because he was a foreigner with a thick accent. Yet they wouldn't think twice about dating any European, French, or Russian man who glanced their way, a fact that always confused him. So he was left with a decision: wait for gorgeous Black American women who didn't seem interested in him to change their minds, or sample the international buffet of equally beautiful women who apparently fawned over him like he was a member of the Beatles. He chose the latter. It was clear that Miss Shinglar had his attention, in no small part because she initially didn't pay him any.

On their first date, he wanted to impress her. With a grand total of $46 in his pocket, he took her to a well-known restaurant in Albany. Credit cards were in their infancy, and $46 was a fair amount of money in those days. Coming from a family where her Uncle George had schooled her in the ways of hunting, Mom naturally ordered the pheasant. In fact, she ordered "pheasant under glass," served under a glass casing to keep the meat moist - unaware that her selection would comprise the majority of the bill. Dad ordered the meatloaf. And for the next couple of hours, these two people from distant, different worlds shared a quiet dinner getting to know each other. By the time they were done, the young physician had about 45 cents to his name, and could only leave a 25 cent tip on a $45 tab. The restaurant staff probably thought he was the cheapest patron to ever dine there, possibly originating the myth of Black people being poor tippers at that very meal. Dad had no desire to make that dubious moment in Black history - he was just trying to impress this young woman who had turned down his advances so many times before. He thought highly of this young Donna Shinglar. She was pure and innocent, with a good head on her shoulders. Most importantly in his mind, he knew she thought of him as just another person. She wasn't racist.

Mom experienced this young Haitian man as a pure gentleman - a far cry from the womanizer she had heard about. He opened doors, was respectful, walked her to the steps of her dormitory, and came off differently than any other dating experience she had up to that point. For someone raised to be scared of and dislike Black people, she was now experiencing first-hand a Black man who treated her with more courtesy and consideration than most of the men in her family ever had. Their first date was good by both of their standards, until Dad attempted to give her a small kiss as he dropped her off.

"How dare you?" she exclaimed. "I don't do that on the first date!"

She left him abruptly, and he felt horrible that he had offended her after what was a perfect first date. By the time Mom had made it back to her dorm room, the hallway phone was ringing. It was Dr. Malebranche, "the gentleman," apologizing for offending her with the kiss and meekly asking for her forgiveness. She did, and the phone call made her feel good that he had respected her wishes.

After that night they began dating more steadily. The highly sought-after Chief Resident was also seeing other young ladies, a fact of which Mom was keenly aware. She understood that sometimes he would drop her off after a date only to pick up another girl, sparking many arguments between them. Like many young romances, they would reach a crossroads and stop dating for a while, only to pick back up again later. All the while, she continued her nursing training and he continued his physician training. Things between them became serious at the end of her junior year when a break-in happened in the Nursing School dorm, prompting the school to hire a private investigator. The investigator uncovered what he viewed as a salacious, interracial love affair, which prompted one of the Nursing School administrators to call the young nurse to her office.

"Miss Shinglar, I'm going to call your aunt and father to let them know you are dating a Black man," she threatened.

The administrator told her that if she were to continue dating this Black surgical resident, her children would be bastards and she would be a disgrace to the school. Mom offered to resign her spot in her class, but they wouldn't accept. They never executed their threat to tell her family that she was dating a Black man. Unfortunately, another nurse from Granville working in Schenectady also disapproved of her relationship with Dr. Malebranche, so word spread back to Granville anyway. Her Aunt Anna, the very same aunt who put her to work at the summer camp years ago, sent a caustic letter informing Mom that her father had disowned her.

At the same time, Dad was growing increasingly concerned about his two children, Roger Jr. and Marie Christine, the offspring of a previous relationship with a White woman.

Standing on His Shoulders

In the 1960s, biracial children born out of wedlock were commonly considered bastards or illegitimate. After discussing things with Mom, and feeling he should do the right thing by his children, he decided to marry his children's mother in New York with plans to divorce her immediately afterwards. This would at least give his children some legitimate standing in society.

Roger Malebranche was in love now, and his two precious children were the only reason he was in contact with this woman from his past. New York State law would not acknowledge the divorce, so Dad had to travel to Mexico where they could formally complete the divorce paperwork. Immigration officials blocked his return to the United States, citing student visa restrictions which only allowed one reentry into the county. Since he had already used that after returning from Haiti when Tante Jeanne died, they detained him in Mexico.

Mom, recently disowned by her own family, was newly pregnant with my sister Michelle, and ready to start her own. She ventured to Mexico by herself to bring Dad money and help him get back to the United States. That was the first time she had ventured out of upstate New York, the first time she flew on a plane, and the first time she set foot in another country. Yes, this woman from Granville truly loved this man from Anse-à-Veau. The two star-crossed lovers married in the quaint, northern Mexican town of Guadalupe in October 1966, spending their honeymoon there in a budget hotel. The newly minted Mrs. Malebranche left Mexico to return to Schenectady in 1967. There she secured political support from his surgical mentors at Ellis Hospital and worked with a Texas lawyer to navigate her husband's safe return to New York. Dr. Malebranche had just accepted a position as a surgical teaching fellow at St. Clare's Hospital in Schenectady, which was willing to help him get back in the U.S. The whole process took six months. Dad returned to the operating room, this time as a husband.

For the next few years, Mom remained estranged from her Granville home and didn't speak to anyone. Communication with her father was entirely cut off by his choice, and he was frequently in and out of hospitals due to congestive heart failure. She knew he didn't want to see or hear from her, all because she had married a Black man. Mom never resented him for his blind racist anger, but she would never speak with the man she knew as her father again. In 1972 Basil Shinglar died from complications of heart failure. His one daughter who had left years earlier as a naïve and sheltered teenager now returned to Granville as a wise, twenty-six-year-old woman, wife, and mother of two. She stood alone for her father's funeral, not wanting to subject her husband and children to any prejudicial ill will. She paid her respects as any good daughter would – but didn't stay for the reception.

Not long after Mom's father died, so did her Uncle George, another casualty of years of heavy smoking. At the funeral, her Aunt Mary asked her to stop by the house to talk. She had been doing some research on this Black man everyone in Granville was talking about, and discovered that Roger Malebranche was in fact, a good man and respected surgeon. Aunt Mary extended an invitation to bring him to visit Granville one day, but for the former Miss Shinglar, her family had already inflicted enough emotional abuse to last her several lifetimes. She declined Aunt Mary's invitation, not wanting to put her husband and children in Schenectady through any unnecessary drama. Mom cut her ties with Granville except her brother Bill. She now had her own family to love and nurture, and committed herself to ensuring that her children would never feel unwanted for a second of their precious lives.

Son, I knew in my heart that your mother was "the one" from the moment I met her. I had made some terrible mistakes in my relationship with the mother of my first two children. I thought these mistakes would make things difficult with your mother. Tante Jeanne had just died when we met. She stepped into the void that Tante Jeanne's passing left in my heart, as the most important woman in my life was now gone. If she hadn't died, I would've probably moved back to Haiti to marry the young woman who had been chosen to be my wife. And that would have been my destiny. But God decided to bless me with this beautiful woman from Granville, New York — and she would become an amazing wife, mother, friend, and my life companion. She has always been there for me.

When you were young we lived in a small two-story house on Bradley Boulevard during the 1970s. It wasn't much - simple panel siding, three cramped bedrooms, but it was enough. I would return home in the evening after a long shift in the Emergency Room and slowly ascend the walk-up to the front door. My legs were weary, my arms heavy, and I smelled of drugs and antiseptics.

David J Malebranche

When I entered the door, your mother would greet me with a kiss and glance over to the living room. You and Michelle had fallen asleep on the frayed couch in front of the television waiting for me to come home. I would scoop both of you in my arms and carefully walk up the stairs to your bedrooms to put you to bed. As I journeyed up those stairs carrying our precious cargo, your mother was with me for each and every step, arms outstretched in anxious anticipation - ready to catch us and break our fall if I should falter. It was the two of us against the world my son. It has always been. It will always be.

4

WIDE-EYED WONDERMENT

I was five years old when I first watched my father walk on water in hospital corridors. He navigated pristine halls of antiseptic sterility in his tailored two-piece grey suit, showcasing broad shoulders before his wingtip shoes could announce his arrival. Dad was a commanding presence – a confident brown-skinned Black man with perfectly-coiffed short hair, a thick Caribbean accent, and refined mannerism for days. At a standard, yet imposing, six feet tall, he didn't just walk when he conducted hospital rounds; he sauntered across the floor like Haitian royalty.

As the Chief Surgeon of St. Clare's Hospital in Schenectady, New York, Dad would sometimes let me tag along to see him in action. Busy surgical inpatient floors, operating rooms, and the doctors' lounge where the staff changed from dress clothes into their scrubs were all an ample playground of magical mystery to me. He seemed proud to show me every room in his medical kingdom, and people responded to him as if Jesus himself had just entered the building, ready to convert water to wine. It wasn't just the other doctors who were obviously moved by his presence, but the nurses, janitors, phlebotomists, lab techs, and other staff as well. He recalled their names and, with a warm smile, gentle handshake, or touch on the shoulder, would inquire about their families and intimate details of their personal lives. It was as if each co-worker was the only person he had ever known. When he introduced me, they beamed and acted as if I was one of their own children – affectionately patting me on the head and exclaiming how lucky I was to be Dr. Malebranche's son. My eyes ballooned with amazement that this man holding my hand was *my father*. I felt like I was walking with the King of the hospital. In many ways, I was.

Dad drove a bright red, stick shift Volkswagen Beetle that was all the rage in the 1970s. From within the safe confines of the rigid passenger seat, I marveled at how effortlessly he handled that automobile. How he deftly manipulated the clutch with one hand while prodding the accelerator with his feet was nothing short of masterful. The cylindrical machine always responded instinctively, jerking and pulling us forward like a rickety roller coaster. No matter how bumpy the ride was, I always felt protected while the melodious strains of Vivaldi, Bizet, or other classical music serenaded my ears. As time passed, the Volkswagen morphed into a more contemporary steely black Saab Turbo, with just a little more punch and kick than its rose-kissed predecessor. Throughout it all, Dad was in control, and I was in awe. I felt like I was the luckiest kid alive.

I was blessed to have many good memories of Dad growing up. On some Saturday mornings he would wake up early with me and watch Saturday morning cartoons like *Johnny Quest, The Justice League*, or *Scooby Doo*. I greedily devoured Frosted Flakes or Apple Jacks in my one-piece pajamas, engrossed by the animated storyline of that week and comforted by having my father lying near me. During summer vacations, he would wake me up at 5 a.m. so we could go fishing together on Sacandaga Lake. At holiday times, Dad wouldn't have anyone else attempt to carve Mom's golden brown turkey. I would often peek over the kitchen counter and watch him guide the buzzing carving knife with surgical precision as it sliced us perfectly-sized portions for consumption. Occasionally Dad would take me to fly kites in Central Park. He would help me put it together, then hold the spool of string and urge me to run with the brightly colored aircraft in my hand. And run I did, frenetically darting up and down the uneven grass until I could feel the wind licking at my fingers as I let go. The kite would then take on a life of its own, soaring through the sky in celebration of its newfound freedom. As I returned to Dad, he would hand me the anchor of thread so I could resume running to and fro, pulling the kite wherever I went. It was true teamwork, and best of all it was with him.

Dad was also a man's man, and carried himself with a very traditional masculine swagger that could be intimidating but never scary. He was a fierce disciplinarian; rarely raising his voice, but when he did you knew you were in trouble. He and Mom firmly believed that curfews existed for a reason, playtime was reserved until all schoolwork was complete, and, if discipline was called for, ass-whoopings could be administered without any advance notice. If my sister Michelle or I had done anything bad, disrespectful, or out of pocket, Dad wouldn't have to say a word. His eyes would narrow ever so slightly as he called us to him and simultaneously started reaching for his belt. And with Pavlovian instincts, we would scatter like roaches, but never quick enough to escape his grasp as he yanked us out of the air like ragdolls and flipped us over his knee in one smooth motion. The only question in either of our minds would be whether the spanking would be over the pants, over the underwear, or bare ass. To me it was all the same – belts stung no matter how many layers of clothes you had on. The balance of affection and discipline growing up in the Malebranche household kept me out of trouble on most days. Mom and Dad loved us, but the message was crystal clear – they were our parents, not our friends.

As I grew older, my memories of Dad became more selective and increasingly pejorative in nature. Instead of recollecting the quality time we did share and how he cared enough to discipline me, I grew accustomed to frustrated remembrances of how much Dad worked and wasn't at home. Mornings, evenings, weekends, and even holidays – he never stopped working. His hospital schedule was an incessant interruption in our family life, preventing him from attending numerous sporting events and school activities in which my sister and I were engaged. Many times I was awakened in the middle of the night from a deep sleep by the intrusive ringing of the phone, the hospital operator calling him about a patient in need. His booming footsteps would then trudge past my bedroom to the shower, a ritual meant to wake him up. Moments later more deliberate footsteps moved past my bedroom door, trailed by the converging scents of Ivory soap and Lubriderm lotion, as he prepared to take care of the surgical emergency du jour. On most of those days Dad was pulled from his slumber in the early morning hours, we wouldn't see him until the evening for dinner, and sometimes not before we went to bed. It was just a dynamic that grew to be accepted as the norm by the entire family.

I was jealous of my father's job. She was the part-time lover that took him far and away from witnessing my baseball games, football games, and track meets. She received the majority of his attention, draining him of all his energy so that there was little to share with his family when he came home. Many days after dinner he would retreat to the basement for hours, working in solitude on clocks and watches until we were all ready for bed. While I understood the nature of the demanding life of a surgeon, it nonetheless left an indelible impression on me. The time he spent with us, a few sparse hours in the same house while he worked alone, didn't resemble quality time in any way, shape, or fashion. Dad's work unapologetically pulled his time and attention closer to his patients and further away from his family. My resentment of her presence was palpable. I couldn't fully comprehend how her existence, albeit unwanted by me, was necessary to keep a roof over our heads.

Despite the lack of physical time Dad spent with us growing up, he made gestures to ensure we knew he was present when he was home. Every morning before he left and every evening before he went to bed, he would kiss Michelle and me on the cheek or forehead in a ritualistic fashion. Similarly, after every amazing dinner my mother prepared, he would rise from his chair, slowly walk over to her, kiss her lovingly on the lips or cheek and say "thank you Mom." These expressions were subtle and constant reminders that when he was physically present, he was emotionally present as well. He was putting himself through all those long hours, late nights and early morning interruptions so that his family could live a better life.

In 1968, Michelle was only a year old, and my mother was carrying me in her womb. Dad was trying to make ends meet working as a teaching fellow in surgery, monitoring the new interns at St. Clare's Hospital while simultaneously moonlighting as a surgical assistant. His hours were long, his monthly income was $500, and Mom didn't see him much. Their cramped upstairs apartment sat directly across the street from the hospital. It was both convenient and just enough space in which our young family could exist as a cozy unit. Winter was particularly harsh in Schenectady that year. The snow was relentless in its persistence, breaking limbs off trees, suffocating cars in the street, and making routine day-to-day activities challenging and miserable.

Dad was working so hard and often that he had worn his favorite winter coat down to a tattered piece of cloth barely capable of providing insulation. Mom decided to put aside some money and, just before Christmas, gave it to him on his day off so he could buy himself a new coat. He spent hours away from home, making her worried that something bad had happened to her young husband. Later that evening he returned home, proudly sporting the same flimsy coat, but carrying a brand new teddy bear in his hand. The stuffed animal was a glowing golden mass of fur and movable appendages, the kind that makes growling noises when you shake it just right. He had spent hours looking for a new coat in many different stores, but as soon as his eyes caught a glimpse of that plush beast in the department store display case, it was over. All he could think about was how much more his one-year-old daughter would enjoy that bear than he would relish having a new coat. So he bought the bear. And my mother, unable to be angry with him, started another savings plan for a cold, winter day.

I'm sure my father wished he could have worked and spent time with us simultaneously, but it just wasn't physically possible. He put his family first because he was raised to embrace the notion that a good man is a good provider. I didn't always understand that as a child. I just wanted to spend time with my Dad.

5

CALL THEM WHITE TRASH

For a few summers during my childhood, our family would take a trip to a summer house on Sacandaga Lake in upstate New York for a week or two of vacation. The days were gorgeously lazy, filled with early morning fishing trips with my Dad, swimming with my sister and mother, and timeless moments away from the daily pressures of life. The quaint, dilapidated house sat on a hill overlooking the water, smelling of mothballs and the benign elderly neglect of the pastor who rented it to us. Living there was like a time warp in which only the barest living essentials were offered: a flimsy wooden roof over our heads, adequate plumbing, a small gas stove, and numerous screen doors to keep the mosquitoes outside where they belonged. For middle school-aged me, there was nothing to do there. Left to my own devices, I would create whatever fun was to be had – catching fireflies in a see-through jar, burning ants on the pavement with a magnifying glass, and swimming in the cloudy lake for hours on end. The abundance of time-wasting activities I had at my disposal was endless.

The down time at that lake also afforded me transient glimpses into seeing Dad actually looking relaxed. He would spend most of his days gleefully curled up on his bed, his eyes slicing through the latest Louis L'Amour western novel or collection of short stories. Reading was his stress release, his main extracurricular activity, and something which I never fully understood. To me, reading was a chore, a mind-numbing exercise designed to feign intellectual pursuit. All I really wanted to do was play video games. Reading represented an entirely different thing for Dad. It was how he chose to decompress from the drama of chaotic surgery schedules, busy patient clinic days, and life or death decision-making. It was a necessary aspect of maintaining his sanity.

Sacandaga Lake, with all its picturesque beauty and charm, was also the place where I first met racism. When you're young, it's true that you don't really pay attention to race issues unless someone brings them up. Kids, for the most part, are innocent and generally accepting of superficial differences between them until brainwashed by media or adults. They aren't trying to think about whether other kids are Black or White, Latino, Asian, or Native American. They're just trying to eat, play, and sleep. It's that simple. And my parents, despite having experienced their fair share of discrimination for being an interracial couple, weren't trying to put their own children in compartmentalized racial boxes. They wanted

Michelle and me to be accepted, regardless of how we looked or who our parents were. As my father often proclaimed *"Son, there's only one 'race' – the human race."*

The day I met racism was no different than any other. I was playing with a few neighbors, other kids who spent summers on the lake with their families like we did. The serene water reflected the radiant sun, and the aroma of processed hot dogs and grilled hamburgers wafted through the country air. We were engaged in activities kids do on restless warm days: playing games, making fun of each other, calling out silly names like "doo-doo face," "dummy," "jerk," and "idiot." These were all the insults you thought could hurt someone's feelings, but really had the emotional impact of a marshmallow. Suddenly, out of one boy's lips flew a word that shot through the hot, summer air and struck me squarely in my face like a brass-knuckled fist, piercing my virginal eardrums so violently that we all knew playtime was over.

"Nigger!" he spewed.

The word was said with such a venomous hatred and contempt that I had to wipe its aerosolized filth off my face. I had no idea what it meant but the abrasive sound of it made me immediately stop playing. He said it repeatedly with extra vigor to make sure I heard him correctly.

"Nigger, nigger, nigger!" he chanted.

The other kids just laughed, and I stood there, exposed and helpless to fight back against a word whose meaning I struggled to comprehend. A large cloud now hovered over Sacandaga Lake, and I returned to the house with my head held low and my tail between my legs. I fully understood that

I was being insulted in a particularly derogatory manner, but I longed to know the meaning of this new word, and more importantly, why it bothered me so much. I knew only one person could provide me with answers – Dad, the well-read man and widely respected surgeon who knew everything. He would know what the strange word meant. So that night after dinner, as he was relaxing reading a book, I approached him.

"Dad, what does 'nigger' mean?" I asked.

He put down his book and looked at me. His face, usually smooth and devoid of any wrinkles that would indicate the slightest hint of strain – was now twisted on itself in anger and concern. It was probably a conversation he wished he wouldn't have to have with me, but here we were.

"Who called you that son?" he asked calmly.

"This kid at the lake."

Dad sat me up in front of him and looked me directly in my eyes with an intensity I rarely saw. Class was about to begin.

"When you see that kid tomorrow, and if he calls you a 'nigger' again, I want you to call him 'white trash'."

"White trash?" I said, now even more confused by my father's proposed retort than the insult I didn't even recognize. I repeated "white trash" several times in my head and aloud, using different tones and inflections, to see if it had the same sharp bite as "nigger." It didn't. When the phrase left my mouth, it simply fell flaccid like a wet noodle on the floor. I guess I could've just called him "stupid head," "fart face," or any other variety of juvenile insults I typically relied upon in these crucial situations. In the game of verbal name calling, I was certain to get my ass kicked. I trusted that Dad knew best, so even if it didn't sound right, I was going to use it anyway and make that kid regret he ever fixed his pale thin lips to call me "nigger" in the first place.

Sure enough, the next day, amidst a different backdrop of blue skies and cumulus clouds, I mixed it up with the same group of kids. The same racist brat triumphantly returned like some poorly looped audio recording.

"Nigger!" he shouted.

This time I was ready for him, and I shot him with the verbal ammunition directly passed down to me from my wise father.

"White trash!" I hollered.

Silence descended as I stood at defiant attention, waiting for him to fall back and recoil in deference to my obvious knockout punch. Instead he just looked at me, laughed, called me "nigger" again, and ran off with the rest of the kids. Even though I had stood up for myself, lashed back at him, and used the exact words Dad had taught me, somehow I still felt defeated. It wasn't until later when I learned the historical significance of the word "nigger" – a word derived from a Latin root simply referring to black color, yet appropriated by racist slave owners to demean and dehumanize people of African descent. A word that has persisted and mutated over centuries long enough to be reclaimed by Black people ourselves. A word we often use to describe each other as a curious hybrid term-of-endearment and self-deprecation. In historical context, my "white trash" retort never stood a chance.

My experience at the lake was merely an introductory course on race. I later learned that for the biracial kids of this world - the "mulattoes," "high yella," or "half-breeds" as we are sometimes affectionately called, other kids would pigeonhole us into a racial category, based on our physical features. Genetic composition doesn't matter as much as external appearance when people are making snap assessments of who you are. The darker your skin hue, the more likely you will be perceived as Black, and the more racial discrimination you will undoubtedly experience. These experiences, in turn, shape our racial identities and how we see ourselves positioned in this society. And along the racial hierarchy of desirability and social status, I have witnessed many mixed race people who longed to be anything but Black. Whether it was the actress Rae Dawn Chong, golfer Tiger Woods, or the ubiquitous clown who is always around to proudly announce "I have Indian in my family," there are copious illustrations of multiracial people who go to outrageous lengths to define themselves as anything but Black. For a biracial, bicultural kid in upstate New York, finding examples of multiracial people who actually affirmed their Blackness was like finding the proverbial needle in a haystack. My experience, however, has been quite different. I became quite clear of who I was and how the world saw me after that summer at Sacandaga Lake. I chose not to run from my Blackness. I embraced it.

Growing up in Schenectady, practically all of my classmates at school were White. There were only a handful of Black students in middle school through high school. Some

White classmates viewed me through that classic cliché of "you're not like other Blacks" and were actually bold enough to verbally tell me so. To them, I wasn't dark enough and surely didn't fit the stereotype of what they thought being Black was: I spoke intelligently, was only an average basketball player, and lived in a middle class section of town not known for its rough and tumble proclivities. Others would forget I was present as the word "nigger" would carelessly escape their lips in routine conversation, only to quickly retract it with an "oops, sorry Dave." Others would even whisper popular Black jokes circulating within their families to each other while I was present as if I couldn't hear. Some even felt comfortable enough to tell these jokes while sitting in our house, and would label me as sensitive or radical if I called them on it. They didn't seem to grasp how much it hurt me for them to call me friend yet harbor those kinds of prejudiced sentiments. And how could they? Privilege oozed from their pores, trickled carelessly down their foreheads, and muddled their vision with a thin veil that even they didn't know was there. They chose not to see me. I was invisible to them. Sometimes I was even invisible to myself.

I've had more than my fair share of encounters with racism and discrimination since those days in Schenectady and Sacandaga Lake. They have been both blatant and subtle, altogether transcendent beyond merely being called a "nigger." In high school, I was pulled over by police simply for driving a Saab, my father's car at the time. The officer politely informed me that the car was "too nice" for me to be driving after clocking me at an obscene five miles per hour under the speed limit. In college, campus police stopped me repeatedly to show school ID while simply walking across campus or after receiving reports of a suspicious man carrying crates of vinyl records to my radio show. In medical school, White hotel patrons in North Carolina and Texas mistook me for a hotel shuttle driver and a parking valet while wearing a 3-piece suit before two separate medical residency interviews. During medical residency in New York City, an older White male patient with no history of dementia asked me if I was the cable TV repairman when I walked into his room. I was wearing a clearly visible hospital ID badge, white coat, and stethoscope around my neck. While none of these microaggressions are exactly the same as being called a "nigger" outright, they still cut with the same ferocity. They have served as a constant and painful reminder of how larger society may often see me, regardless of how many degrees I have, how much money I make, the number of accomplishments I achieve, or the kind of professional attire I wear. I'm thankful every day that I didn't make the "white trash" insult part of my verbal repertoire. Using it as a common slur would reduce me to nothing more than the racists whom I claim to detest.

Being called a "nigger" at a very young age helped mold and cement my Black racial identity, despite my parents' efforts to raise me as a raceless biracial child. It was curious to me how Dad didn't directly address the trauma of my being called that hateful word at such a young age. Perhaps he knew in his heart that raising me in a tradition of normative Black excellence, an ignorant six-letter word couldn't touch me. So in a brilliant way and without ever explaining to me exactly what the word "nigger" meant, he used the moment as a teaching opportunity. This wasn't a lesson in how to shield myself from the trauma of racism. It was a lesson in how to stand up for myself and how *not* to turn the other cheek.

Even as a child, I knew that "nigger" was a special kind of bad word before I understood its history. So instead of focusing on the word itself, Dad redirected my thoughts to the general importance of fighting back and defending myself when someone picks on me. Even though the "white trash" kid insulted me again and didn't seem to be phased by my retaliation, I realized that I would never back down to anyone who used that word or any other racial slur against me. No matter how the external world saw me, I would have the confidence to not allow these racial insults to have power over me to the point where I would think lesser of myself. When I am faced with a situation where racism may rear its hideous head, I don't stoop to calling people "white trash" or engage in pointless name-calling. Nor do I sit in awkward silence and passively wait for the uncomfortable moment to pass. Instead, I choose to be vocal in my recognition of and opposition to it, all the while clear that it will never permeate my psyche or paralyze my forward progress. The best response to racism is to continue to succeed and go toward the destiny planned for me. That is, and will always be, the biggest and brightest insult I can throw back at it.

6

WHY DIDN'T YOU GET 100?

Anyone raised in a West Indian household understands the meaning of hard work. The Wayans brothers mocked our work ethic in the 1990s sketch comedy TV show *In Living Color*, in which they portrayed members of a West Indian family. Each member held down at least three jobs and looked down on anyone who only had one. For those who thought that was an exaggeration or stereotype, think again. Growing up with my father, the focus was very much on education and productivity. Nothing short of excellence was expected of you. If you didn't live up to those expectations, your desire and motivation were questioned.

Dad never showed even the faintest interest in our participation in sports or other extracurricular activities in school. Michelle would score twenty-five points for her high school basketball team and nary an eyebrow would be raised. I got a touchdown and interception in my football game but barely a yawn escaped his lips. In his mind, our grades and academic achievements were the only things that mattered - all other activities were blatantly secondary. Mom, however, was the quintessential nurturer and supporter in the Malebranche household. She was "Team David" or "Team Michelle" without question, regardless of what extracurricular activity we chose to pursue. I remember her being there for my track meets with a smile and hug to tell me I did a good job, no matter how well I placed. She was there to pick me up and drop me off for every baseball, basketball, and football game. She stayed and cheered me on whether I was playing or not, and regardless of how well I played. She held me and consoled me when I didn't make the 8th grade basketball team. She made sure my team uniforms were always cleaned and ready every time I took to a field or court. She meticulously prepared brown bag meals and took Michelle and me to McDonald's after games to make sure we had enough sustenance. Yes, Mom had high expectations for us like my father did, but she did it with flair and a safety net to catch us if we fell during our ascent. She made sure that for all of our childhood activities and milestones, at least one of our parents would be present to bear witness. Regardless of the outcome, she was always there to make sure we knew we were loved. Mom provided balance and a reminder that academics were important, but not the only thing in life.

During high school, I learned an important lesson about Dad's priorities when it came to academics and extracurricular activities. Up until that point, I was going to class, coming home, and doing my homework. I coasted through my studies doing the bare minimum in order to maintain peace in the Malebranche household. My reputation for treading water was legendary, and as natural as the oxygen that flowed through my lungs. On average, I typically scored between 94 and 100 on most of my tests and exams, a solid "A" by anyone's definition. I was also playing football, basketball, running cross country, and participating in student government. Most outside observers would have viewed me as an active and well-rounded student.

As with any high school class, there were other students who focused solely on academics and pulled a 99 average every quarter. One of my classmates, Francis Alcedo, was one such student. He fit the description of what many would consider a nerd in the 1980s – short and slight of frame, soft-spoken, with thick Coke bottle glasses. He was pleasant enough with a quiet demeanor, seen by some as socially awkward, and his main activity was editing the school yearbook. I always felt it was pretty easy for Francis to score 99 or 100 on every test since it didn't appear that he did anything but study. Unfortunately for me, our fathers knew each other, and it got back to Dad that Francis reportedly felt I was an underachiever in school. Not only that, but he also felt that if I focused more on my studies instead of sports and other activities, I could get a 99 average just like he did. Obviously, since all he had in his daily life was his schoolwork, he had a lot of time to make detailed observations about my academic motivation and how hard I was working. Of course, I never heard Francis say any of this, but this was what Dad had heard. Truth or not, I was gonna catch hell.

I began to feel like the only underachiever with a 95 average. Every evening, for what seemed like weeks, Dad put a thick heaping of Haitian guilt on my daily dinner plate, lamenting over how embarrassed he felt that my classmate had assessed me as a slacker. Truth be told, if Francis had said those things, he was actually right. I was skating carelessly through school, putting forth just enough effort to do well, but not reaching my full potential. And maybe that's why I never approached him about the validity of what my father heard. I knew it was true regardless of whether he had said it or not. I just didn't like someone else pointing out my hustle, and my initial immature high school reaction to the situation was typical. I convinced myself that I really didn't give a shit about it because Francis had nothing more than a high GPA going for him. I preferred my status as jack-of-all trades with a 95 average rather than a one-trick-pony with a 99. Francis' reported comments, while not malicious in their intent, were a very personal attack on my character, integrity, and family. He obviously had limited understanding of the internal wiring of a Haitian father, and how this father would respond to such an assessment of his youngest son.

The more I thought about it, however, the more motivated I became beyond knee-jerk teenage apathy. Francis, unbeknownst to him, had just laid down the gauntlet. This was a challenge I was prepared to accept. Anyone who truly knows me understands that if you think I can't do something, I'm going to do it just to prove that I can. Whether writing a grant, publishing a manuscript, taking care of a complicated patient, or simply being told that I couldn't possibly eat a large pepperoni pizza by myself - if you say I can't do it, I will. So I took his allegation about my motivation to heart, and challenged myself to be more academically competitive that semester. My goal was a 99 GPA or bust. Despite continuing to participate in all my other school and extracurricular activities, I spent more time studying and became beastly efficient with homework. Even though I already had a curfew, I made sure I didn't engage in unnecessary activities that could distract me from my studies. When the smoke cleared, I emerged from that semester with a 97 overall GPA for all my classes. I was disappointed that I didn't get the 99, but I realized two things: First, it was hard as hell to raise an overall GPA from a 95 to a 97. Second, I was able to maintain a higher average despite doing all the same extracurricular activities, simply by working harder. Go figure.

For Dad, however, being a well-balanced student wasn't the goal, what mattered was the grade. This was the objective evidence of success that no amount of subjectivity, personal bias, or racial predilection could ever take away from me. Francis' alleged comment had hurt Dad's pride and he saw it as a slight on his competence as a father. Nothing short of me getting a higher GPA than Francis himself would have satisfied him. Dad spent his childhood with the expectation that he would always be the top student in his class. He would tell me stories of scoring lower on a test than one of his White classmates in Haiti, to which Tante Jeanne would sternly ask him, "How could you let that stupid White kid beat you?"

His mentality and the expectations under which he was raised were the inverse of societal expectations of young Black men in America. The message wasn't a blanket generalization that White people were all unintelligent, but rather that Black people were cerebral equals, if not better. For Dad, being second just wasn't good enough, and Black excellence was the rule, not the exception.

Not fully understanding this context, I walked into our living room one night, wrapped warmly in my naiveté and pride from my current report card. Dad sat peacefully in his rocking chair after a long day of work, playing his Nintendo Gameboy to sharpen up his hand-eye coordination for surgery. I handed the report card to him. He put down his device, adjusted his glasses, and slowly, deliberately perused my improved grades. I was frozen with anxious anticipation of his reaction to my hard work. When he finished, he took his glasses off, handed the report card back to me and gave me a deadpan look.

"Why didn't you get 100?" he queried.

For a moment I thought maybe I had just heard him wrong. He surely wasn't asking me why I didn't get a 100 average on all my classes after all the work I had done to get a 97. Naw, I just heard him wrong.

"What?" I replied like I didn't hear him the first time.

"Why didn't you get 100?" he shot back at me sternly as if to say, "Did I stutter?"

My spirit was broken, and I wasn't even remotely prepared to answer his question. I had anticipated that 1980s Bill Cosby moment where, in his ugly colorful Coogi sweater and warm vocal tone, the good Doctor Huxtable looks at Theo and says, "This is great son, I'm so proud of you." That's what I felt I needed to hear after a long hard school semester. "Why didn't you get 100?" is the last question that should be on a father's mind when his son brings home a report card with a 97 average! What kind of twisted father torments his kids by expecting perfection from them without even acknowledging when they do something good? Dejected, I just took the report card back and retreated to the kitchen. Dad, not realizing the impact of the words he just uttered, merely adjusted his glasses and returned to helping Dr. Mario arrange his multicolored pills as they haphazardly dropped from the sky.

This was not the last time Dad would brush off what I felt were significant accomplishments. In my sophomore year of high school, I took the Preliminary Scholastic Aptitude Test (PSAT), a practice test for the official SAT. The SAT is the standardized test that high school students take in preparation for college applications, and in many cases, sets the standard by which they are judged as to whether they have the academic ability to perform in some of the nation's top colleges. The top score you could get back then was 1600, but most people considered anything over 1100 competitive.

Of course, being an "always able to get A's but never quite living up to my potential" 15-year-old, I didn't prepare for the PSAT at all. I thought I could take it cold turkey and just do well. My life was more interesting when I threw spitballs at people, put tacks on classmates' seats as they took their chairs, and made smart mouth comments to cranky old teachers who put too much Vaseline in their hair. Most of my instructors hated me because they could never tell me that my disruptive behavior was causing my grades to slip. They would utter, "You know Mr. Malebranche, just because you get good grades doesn't give you the right to distract everyone else!" Yeah, I was *that* kid – the one who thought he could just keep skating by, distracting anyone I desired. As long as I maintained good grades with minimal effort, I didn't care what they thought of me.

Then I took the PSAT. I tanked the test with a score of 910, not bad by some standards, but definitely not up to par for a teenager accustomed to getting straight A's and the son of an immigrant Haitian father. Other students in my class had scored much higher than I did, and my underachieving performance woke me from my slumber of mediocrity. I knew I had messed up this time, and didn't even need Dad to tell me how poorly I had done. I was disappointed in myself and knew I wasn't performing to the best of my abilities.

Without my parents even nudging me, I bought a small handheld prep book for the SAT, one that included numerous lessons in English, grammar, spelling, and math. For the next year I studied my ass off, worked outside of the classroom, toiled late into the evening, and took innumerable practice SAT tests until I vomited letters, numbers, and multisyllabic words that I would never use in everyday life. By the time the SAT came around early in my junior year, I was ready for it. While I didn't get a perfect score, I did get an 1170, a full 260 points higher than my dismal PSAT performance. As a result, I was awarded a New York Regents Scholarship. These were given to local high school students performing over 1100 on

Standing on His Shoulders

the SAT and would aid in paying for college tuition if you chose to study in New York State. Only 4 people in my class achieved this honor, including myself (and yes, Francis too).

So again I go to my father - the only man who, in my eyes, I longed to make proud and whose approval mattered. I was personally satisfied with how I had raised my SAT score, particularly because I had done it on my own. This time, I saw with my own eyes how I wasn't living up to my potential, and I had proactively done something to fix it. Yet in an eerily familiar déjà vu moment, Dad was again sitting in his beloved antique rocking chair, reading a book while the television sputtered white noise in the background. I handed him the award certificate for the Regents Scholarship, beaming from ear to ear in gleeful anticipation of his affirmation. Instead, he looked it over with a glaze in his eyes, handed it back to me and sighed, "That's great son," and went back to his book. I walked away, dejected again, but fully understood the message. Dad's definition of excellence was higher than mine, and it would take much more than an improved SAT score to get his full attention.

Even as an adult, when I visit my parents and show them an article I've recently published, an award I've received, or a distinction I have been granted, my father still has the same nonchalant response. In 2006 at the ripe age of 37, I was nominated to be on the President's Advisory Council on HIV/AIDS, a committee of experts in the HIV field who help shape U.S. domestic and international policies for the President of the United States. I was certain that recognition on a national level would catch Dad's eye, as he always

53

encouraged me that the best way to do important work in the Black community was to change policy on a larger scale. And this was an honor for which many congratulated me and noted how impressive it was for me to achieve that level of recognition in my field at such a young age.

Instead of spewing effusive compliments in my direction, Dad politely glanced up from his newspaper and looked me in the eye.

"You know son, the key to making an impact in the HIV field is to be more involved on the international level."

I watched his mouth move in slow motion during his proclamation, and seriously considered that even if I replaced Kofi Annan as head of the United Nations it would not matter. He would probably say, "You know son, to really have an impact in this life, you have to lead from the intergalactic level and represent the Universe as leader of the Planet Earth." The standard of success and achievement for a Malebranche has always been an ever-shifting bar. When you get to one level, suddenly that isn't good enough anymore and you have to reach higher, apparently dissatisfied with the current achievement. It took me many years, but I realized that in this game, I could never win. At some point, I was just going to have to be content with my accomplishments on their own, without seeking external validation.

As Dad left the room to work on some watches, unaware of how he had just summarily dismissed me, I looked at my mother who chuckled out of sympathy and understanding. She had witnessed this dynamic for decades and knew that his comment didn't mean he wasn't proud of me. He just had always expected me to achieve great things. In his mind, when his son succeeds like he is *expected* to, this is not a cause for celebration. This is not dissimilar to when a father boldly proclaims, "I take care of my kids!" as if this act in and of itself deserves a gold star. Of course you are expected to take care of your kids – you fathered them! Mom told me not to worry about how my Dad responds directly to me when discussing my work, because she has witnessed him many times tell his close friends and colleagues how proud he is of me, often retelling my accomplishments to the finest detail. So despite his muted response when we are together, my mother would always reassure me that he was proud of me. He just may not always tell me to my face. I've grown to learn that on my own, but it was always reassuring to me to actually hear it.

If it wasn't for my mother's nurturing and supportive advice to affirm me, striving to meet Dad's high expectations probably would have driven me crazy. The style of parenting she employed with me and Michelle was in stark contrast, yet wildly complementary to that of my father's. For every "Why didn't you get 100?" and nonchalant dismissal of our achievements by him, she was there with a kiss or hug to soothe the bitter sting of hurt feelings. Both styles were their own. Both styles were necessary. His for constantly reminding us of the unlimited potential we had, and hers to remind us that the world would not end if we fell short of this potential. Mom's attention to that detail and the nurturing manner in which she provided balance to Dad's high expectations has made all the difference in the world to me.

David J Malebranche

As an impressionable child, I didn't understand why nothing I did was good enough for Dad. As I got older, I learned to understand and appreciate what a blessing it is to have high expectations of young Black males as my father had of me. I am the product of my upbringing whether I like it or not, whether I realize it or not. The expectations Dad had of me were merely reflections of his upbringing in Anse-à-Veau. Tante Jeanne would tell him, "Blan moun sot," ("White people are stupid') if he came in second place academically to the White, French kid in his class. She taught him how to take pride in the normalcy of Black intelligence and high achievement. Tante Jeanne would never show up for Dad's soccer games when he was young. Sports were child's play to her and not worthy of her time. Instead, she would stay up with him as he studied late into the night just to be there, and rolled around on the floor in blissful jubilation after finding out he was the top student in his class. Academic achievements, not athletic prowess, are what made her heart soar. She systematically and repeatedly reinforced the notion of high expectations as an intelligent, young, Black man, while also preparing him for how the world may not validate and affirm him in the nurturing way his home country would. Tante Jeanne knew in her heart that no one could outperform her son, which is probably an expectation every parent should have of their children.

When Dad came to America in the 1960s, in the midst of all the blatant racism towards, and low expectations of, Black men in this country, he came wrapped in an invisible cloak of confidence. It protected him daily and reassured him that he was just as good as anyone else, regardless of their race or ethnicity. When police stopped and harassed him about what he was doing driving a car with "MD" on the license plate, he wasn't bothered. When his White medical colleagues wouldn't refer their surgical patients to him because they were uncomfortable with him being Black, he never stopped striving to make a name for himself. And even when Black patients told him to his face that they would feel more comfortable going to a White doctor instead of him, he honored their wishes but continued to treat any patient who came through his office door, irrespective of their race or ethnicity. Dad was programmed with this mindset. It was fostered in him by being cradled in the arms of a Black republic that was not granted independence, but *took* their independence. He hails from a country where he was not a racial minority, and where a strong-willed mother always encouraged him to think highly of himself. So when he was rudely greeted with racially-biased low expectations from others in the United States, including other Black people, they rolled off his back. He knew he had the skills to achieve anything he wanted, so external perceptions of his capabilities were irrelevant to him. He knew his worth. He always has.

What I viewed as Dad just being mean and unfair was actually him being a good disciplinarian and instilling in me a drive to be the best at everything I do, something he learned from Tante Jeanne. If it wasn't for the high expectations he instilled in me during my youth, I would've listened to all of the disgruntled guidance counselors and racist academic advisors who suggested that I lower my aspirations along my career journey. I would have heeded the horrible advice that I only apply to a local community college instead of an Ivy League school, and that I get my medical residency training from a small community-based program instead of one strong in clinical care, research, policy, and academics. If it wasn't for my father's voice in my head disputing every low expectation anyone tried to project upon me, I might have actually believed their biased interpretation of my potential.

Conversely, I hope I taught my father how important it is, even when we have high expectations of each other, to provide affirmation when we do accomplish something. As an adult, I told him that when I got a 97 average in high school, it would've been nice to get a pat on the back or a "congratulations" before he told me that I could do better. That way, the bar is still set high, but you don't get the feeling like current accomplishments are being overlooked. Despite feeling this way, I have learned to appreciate Dad's approach for what it is. That part of him may never change. For someone who was raised with the highest expectations placed on him as a child, it is natural to assume that he would use the same approach with his own children. And today, I expect the world of myself, family, friends, colleagues, and any young, Black man I have the privilege to mentor and guide.

In 2010, a second year medical student at Morehouse School of Medicine, Leo Moore, asked me to review his personal statement for residency training applications. His essay was well-written, but generic and impersonal, certainly not representative of how truly exceptional a candidate he was. I called him on a warm Saturday morning to give him feedback.

"Leo, I read your personal statement" I said flatly.

"Yes, Dr. David. What did you think?" He knew what was coming.

"Do you enjoy being mediocre?" I asked him bluntly.

He paused. I knew that wasn't the reaction he had expected "No" he responded.

"Well, that's exactly what you're giving me with this essay."

Leo took a moment to collect himself after my brusque response to his question, and to his credit didn't get defensive. We talked for a half hour and I discovered that he had been talked out of his original essay idea by another advisor at school. His first version told a very personal story of a close friend who had tested HIV positive, and how this inspired him to become interested in Internal Medicine and HIV as a career focus. The version he gave me to read was a boring diatribe that sounded like a college student trying to impress a medical school admissions committee, *not* a medical student trying to gain admission into a prestigious residency training program. It contained cliché after cliché of what he was instructed to say, not what he desired to say. We discussed how he could best change it so that it would be more reflective of who *he* is, not of who his other mentor wanted him to portray himself to be.

Despite me telling him not to send me his rewrite until after the weekend was over, Leo had a revision of his personal statement in my inbox no more than four hours after our conversation. The new and improved essay was so personal and heartfelt that it brought tears to my eyes when reading it. Eight months later, he matched with the residency program of his choice. That's the difference between 97 and 100.

7

Reading Is Fundamental

Like most of America, Dad was, and very much still is, preoccupied with the prestige and reputation of Ivy League schools like Harvard University. For him, Harvard represents the pinnacle of academic achievement in the United States, with its international reputation steeped in pomp and circumstance, folklore, and tradition. The appeal of this university to the sensibilities of a confident, overachieving physician hailing from Anse-à-Veau is self-evident. Growing up, every time a table conversation about college was to be had, Harvard was the only two-syllable word that dared to emerge from Dad's parted lips. Unfortunately for him, being the wise-ass, pseudo-rebellious teenager I was at the time meant that whatever college he would suggest was the same college I would try my best *not* to get into. Despite Dad's best efforts, a harmonious marriage between me and Harvard was never going to happen.

Several years ago, I brought a dear friend of mine, Bernard Owens, to meet my parents on a trip to upstate New York. After their initial conversation, Bernard pulled me to the side.

"Your father – he's like royalty!" he exclaimed. "The way he speaks, his attitude about life… He's obviously a brilliant man."

Then he paused and looked at me curiously.

"What the hell happened to you?"

While Bernard's comment was tongue-in-cheek and I knew he wasn't insulting me, he completely understood some of the fundamental differences between my father and me. Dad likes opera and classical music, is an avid reader, collects antique watches and clocks, and unapologetically ascribes to the ideal that there is only one race of people – the human race. I love hip hop, R&B and house music, hate reading unless it's absolutely necessary for work, watch reality TV like it's going out of style, collect comic books and vinyl records, and firmly believe that race and racism plays a role in most everything in this country. Outside of these differences, we are both very passionate Black men, we are stubborn workaholics, we are full of pride, and we refuse to let anyone tell us what we can and cannot do. My reluctance to read when I was younger, particularly newspapers, was a difference I thought was unimportant. I didn't know how my aversion to ocular enlightenment was going to bite me in the ass until I had my college interview with Harvard University.

In high school, whenever Dad wanted me to read the daily newspaper, I would instinctively go straight to the sports and comic sections. Any news story that dealt with politics and world events I found uninteresting and completely unin-spiring. Reading was a waste of my time, and I wasn't willing to pay attention to anything outside of comics, basketball, football, and baseball. As a teenager, although I was academi-cally solid in school, I helplessly wilted under the peer pres-sure from my friends and other students. Being an avid reader just wasn't cool in my pubescent, myopic worldview.

When I got the letter from Harvard University inviting me to an interview with a local alumnus in Albany, I was ex-cited to say the least. The invitation let me know that Harvard considered me worthy. Plus I knew that my father would be proud. He was predictably ecstatic, and gave me pointers on how I should conduct myself, what to say, and what not to do. By the time my Harvard interview had arrived, I had al-ready completed interviews with Georgetown, Princeton, and Yale, so I felt like a seasoned professional. I was ready for any-thing Harvard's snooty asses would throw at me.

Mom drove me to the corporate office where the inter-view would take place, on the top floor of an imposing con-crete and steel building in downtown Albany. She gave me a kiss for good luck and I made my way inside with my flimsy Oak Tree suit, skinny tie, and hand-me-down briefcase. I felt like a million bucks. As I stepped off the elevator, a frumpy, middle-aged White man came to greet me. After an overly firm handshake, he brought me into his office and prompt-ly sat behind an ornate dark mahogany desk. An enormous window hovering ominously behind the desk completed the indulgent room, providing a breathtaking view of downtown Albany. I sat down in the flimsy folding chair set out for me, and waited for the grilling to begin. You could write a dissertation on interview power dynamics the way that room was set up.

Our conversation was pretty standard for the first fifteen minutes as he fired questions about my academic performance, school activities, and why I thought I was a good fit with Harvard. For every question he threw at me, I responded with a quick and deliberate answer. We were like two boxers, Ali and Frazier, ducking and weaving, throwing punches, going toe-to-toe. He was looking for the chink in my armor or one fatal flaw that would land me on the canvas with the rest of the rejects. I was trying to show him that this skinny, big-haired, biracial kid from Schenectady could spar with the Ivy League boys. My acceptance train to Harvard was on the express service to its last stop when the interviewer suddenly took an interest in my last name.

"Malebranche," he proclaimed in his best affected French accent. "That's not a name you see too commonly. What's the origin?"

"It's a Haitian name," I confidently replied, unsure where he was going with this, but I could sense that my ride was about to get a little bumpy. I securely fastened my seatbelt.

"Really? Are both your parents Haitian?" he queried.

"No, just my father. He was born outside Port-au-Prince. I was born in the United States," I replied.

"That's interesting. So what does he think of what's going on in Haiti right now?" he continued.

You could've heard a pin drop - except for the deafening sound of the train carrying my future being derailed and exploding into a million pieces. It was1986 and anyone who could read, or didn't have their head buried in the sand, knew that Haiti was in the middle of huge, political upheaval. The current dictator, Jean-Claude "Baby Doc" Duvalier, was being exiled after a longstanding tyrannical grip on the Haitian people. The very same Baby Doc who Tante Jeanne taught privately as a child. Haiti was on the front page of every major newspaper, with images of demonstrations, the Tonton Macoutes militia, and relentless civil unrest. Everyone was talking about it. Everyone except me, of course, because I wasn't reading that part of the newspaper. I was too busy perusing how many dunks Patrick Ewing had the night before for the Georgetown Hoyas, or what new antics Calvin and Hobbes were up to in the comic section. This was the first of many moments in my life where I wished I *had* taken my father's advice, but it was too late now. The interviewer was inquiring about a topic of which I knew very little about, and my ticket to Harvard University and meeting my father's ultimate expectations hung in the balance. I froze, knowing he wanted an answer that I couldn't possibly provide. Ice cold beads of sweat started to make their pilgrimage down the nape of my neck to saturate the back of my once crisply-starched dress shirt. I blurted out the first thing that popped into my politically ignorant, non-newspaper reading mind.

"He agrees with it." I answered.

The interviewer paused.

"He... agrees with it?" he said confusedly. He looked dumbfounded, contortions developing on his face saying, "How could this kid of Haitian descent not know what's going on in his father's native country?" I was asking myself the same question as I slid slowly under a rock, or more appropriately under the wreckage of the train to Harvard that had not only derailed and exploded, but apparently was also intent on landing directly on top of me.

"Yeah, he agrees with it," I repeated, this time with added emphasis to make sure he truly understood that I was dumb as a brick.

He paused and sized me up for what seemed like an eternity, his beady eyes burning a hole clear through the back of my empty skull. The lump in my throat must've looked like a bowling ball from where he was sitting.

"Ok. So… where is your mother from? What does she do?" he continued.

And just like that, he shifted gears and moved to lighter fare for this prospective applicant who apparently couldn't keep up with current events – even when they directly pertained to his own heritage. He was done with me, and if you listened closely you could hear the faint sound of a toilet bowl flushing. My father's Harvard aspirations for me were swirling down the drain like the verbal waste that had just carelessly released itself from my mouth.

Everything went downhill from there as the interviewer's attitude rotated 180 degrees. He really wasn't interested in anything else I had to say. My validity as a candidate, much less a human being, was torpedoed by my ignorance about Haiti. I tried my best to salvage the rest of my time with him in that decorative office, but I couldn't recover. I was down for the count, unconscious on the canvas, and would not be getting into Harvard. After the final bell rung, he shook my hand politely, we exchanged pleasantries, and I left. I stepped out of that cold corporate building to face a radiant sky that somehow harkened a slightly dimmer future from when I first walked in an hour before.

My mother, always supportive and loving, was right there to pick me up outside the building. I got in the car and mustered the flimsiest smile I could project given the circumstances.

"How did it go?" She asked optimistically.

"Well, I'm not going to Harvard," I replied. If there was a word to describe simultaneously feeling profoundly disappointed yet strangely pleased, that would encapsulate how I was feeling at that moment. I told her the whole story: the interview, the question, my ignorance about Haiti and current events… everything. I even went as far as to tell her that I was glad the interview didn't go well, because I didn't want to go to Harvard anyway. I knew in my heart that was a lie. Not only would it have pleased me to get into Harvard because my father wanted me to go there, but more importantly, I knew I was good enough to get in. I just didn't make the effort. When the letter of rejection from Harvard came that spring, I acted like I was surprised and told Dad I wasn't sure why they didn't accept me. Truth was, I did, and you can bet by the time that rejection letter found refuge in our mailbox, I was well-versed on the whereabouts of Baby Doc Duvalier and the current state of what was going on in Haiti.

I have since come to enjoy reading the news and keeping up with current events in the years since my Harvard interview. I tested the waters first with newspapers, and currently engage myself with online websites and social media. In retrospect, a lot of the good habits my father was trying to instill in me back then were things that I didn't feel I was ready for at that age. Part of my rejecting these activities was just the overall attitude that many teenagers have. I thought I knew what was best for me and no one was going to tell me any different. It took an embarrassing moment in a college interview to show me that book smarts and good grades are a far cry from being well-read. Out of the fourteen universities to which I applied, I was accepted to all except two of them: Harvard and Brown. I knew exactly why I didn't get into Harvard. So now I listen to National Public Radio (NPR) and keep up on current events from whatever news source I can get my hands on, whether they are related to my personal cultural heritage or not. You never know when the knowledge you gain from reading may come in handy. Call me old, stuffy, whatever the hell you want. At least I'll be informed.

8

How It Feels

College was a great experience for me, both for becoming my own man and for physically getting away from my parents, which ironically brought us closer together. I ended up attending Princeton University, a logical compromise between my father's choice (Yale, since I had screwed up my chances of going to Harvard) and my choice (Georgetown, because Patrick Ewing, my favorite basketball player, was a student there while I was in high school). The day I was scheduled to leave for Princeton was a crisp, fall morning, calm and serene with upstate New York trees boasting iridescent-colored leaves. My mother pulled me aside from the kitchen table to tell me that my father had not slept all night, crying sporadically in his office in anticipation of my departure. He was similarly despondent when my sister left for college a year earlier, but I think this was hitting him harder because I was the youngest son, the last one out of the house. The Malebranche family was about to have an empty nest.

We had breakfast that morning at the same golden wooden table that had sturdily supported our meals, poker games, arguments, and birthday celebrations for years. Its timbered foundation was usually bristling with energy and laughter, but this morning was deathly quiet, burdened by the ominous certainty of change. I knew that any attempt at normal conversation would lead to a lot of tears and drama, and none of us were quite ready for that. After eating, Mom, Michelle, and I efficiently and quietly packed the car, while Dad mysteriously disappeared to the back of his office. He came back a few minutes later, shoulders slumped, standing dejectedly on the back porch. His face was twisted by failed attempts to hold back tears and frequent conspicuous sniffling. I finished loading my last bags and met him as he came down the stairs. We hugged and I felt him quivering in my arms. As I returned to the car he shouted to me.

"You know, son, you could stay here with your parents and be a garbage man and we would still be proud of you."

His tears, previously restrained by an equal mix of will, ego, and pride were now free flowing from his eyes. His comment wasn't meant to be a slight on sanitation workers, and I knew he didn't really mean what he had just said. Maybe every parent loses a bit of reality the moment they realize their children are leaving the house, and they say things they don't really mean in the throes of emotional goodbyes. Would anyone actually believe that the perfectionist, high-achieving,

Haitian physician would be happy with his son being a twenty-something-post-college squatter when he wasn't happy with me getting a 97 grade average in high school? I returned to the porch and hugged him tightly again, crying with him before I climbed into the passenger seat of Mom's car. We pulled out of the driveway and turned the corner towards my new journey. His isolated silhouette in the distance became smaller and smaller.

My years at Princeton were filled with interesting experiences of growth, experimentation, and maturation. The strange irony was that it took me going to one of the Whitest Ivy League institutions in the country for me to further develop a sense of my racial identity as a Black man. There were approximately three hundred Black students within Princeton's 4500 enrollment. Given the small and intimate nature of the Black student body at Princeton, two things happened during my tenure there. First, we developed a sense of shared struggle and community being racial minorities at a predominantly White institution. Second, everyone knew each other's business, for better or for worse. The stories of celebration, drama, conflict, and unity among our tight-knit Black community could fill the pages of a separate book all by themselves. I found mentorship in the forms of brilliant men like Michael Eric Dyson and Floyd Thompkins, brothers who more than understood the unique intersectional pressures of being Black men in Ivy League institutions. While I was geographically distant from the teachings of my father, I was nourished by the caring tutelage of these phenomenal male role models. My emerging adulthood occurred under the watchful eye of the lush, green lawns and gothic architecture of that beautiful campus.

Shared moments with Dad during those years took on a different significance, as our relationship transitioned from father and son to a grown man guiding a young adult into manhood. When he could get off work, he would drive the three hours to Princeton with me after holiday breaks and between semesters. We would speedily pass through the beautiful foliage and landscape of the New York State Thruway and the Garden State Parkway. I remember the trees being so bright and charming, setting a fitting ambiance for our excursions. We would talk, laugh, and reminisce about when I was younger. He would give me advice about school, handling difficult situations with friends, and gently nudge me to pursue the medical profession. The best part of these trips was when we would stop at the local Roy Rogers, twenty minutes away from Princeton's campus, always ordering their fried chicken. To hear my father proclaim how much he loved Roy Rogers' fried chicken was humorous to say the least. Seemingly not content with single-handedly establishing the stereotype of Black people as bad tippers during his first date with Mom, he was also dedicated to cementing myths about our dietary preferences as well. Here was a well-traveled man who spoke four languages fluently, enjoyed fine steaks and wines, and had savored exquisite meals all over the world. Roy Rogers, in the hierarchy of fast food fried chicken, doesn't hold a candle to Popeye's, Church's, or even KFC for that matter. It really didn't make much sense to me. But that wasn't the point. I think you could've served him dog food and he would've been happy, as long as it afforded him some extra time to spend with his son.

During those college years, I called Dad periodically to tell him about the experiences I was having and to thank him repeatedly for his advice that I ignored in high school, but was now realizing had value. On my breaks home from school, he would want me to show him and my mother pictures of my close friends. He would often encourage me to have a racially-diverse group of friends, not only other Black students. He'd remind me that White people had power in America and the only way to achieve that same level of power was through working with them, not by segregating from them. I would quickly respond by reminding him that I was at Princeton University, and that any person I would be associating with would be of the highest caliber, regardless of their color, race, or ethnicity. Just to needle him, I would occasionally ask the rhetorical question, "Why is it necessary to encourage me to nestle myself in the bosom of White America if there's only one 'human race'?" That was how many of our conversations about race went during my college years. For me, I was just happy that there was a close-knit Black community at Princeton. It was a welcome change from my predominantly White high school social circles where I was often viewed as an "exception" and was forced to navigate some awkward prejudicial circumstances. For Dad, it was another experience through which he wished to guide me with words of wisdom to avoid any potential life missteps. Yes, I was a more mature college-aged student but still a wise-ass at heart. I was ready to do and say anything that was the exact opposite of whatever he would tell me.

While at Princeton, I started deejaying as a hobby, and it ended up turning into one of my true loves. In my sophomore year, a junior with a large mop of curly red hair named Arthur was the program director for the university radio station, WPRB. He graciously accepted my pitch that Princeton's alternative radio station would benefit from a Hip-Hop/R&B-formatted show. During high school an Albany DJ named "The Candyman," who was reported to be legally blind, hosted a show called Contemporary Soul that inspired me. It was through him that I was exposed to the sounds of Cherelle, Doug E. Fresh, Lisa Lisa & Cult Jam, Eric B & Rakim, Alexander O'Neal, and New Edition. I wanted to do the same for Princeton. When Arthur gave me a radio time slot on Saturday nights from 9pm to midnight, I jumped at the opportunity. I initially thought it was a highly coveted slot, until I realized that most people in college are out partying from 9pm to midnight on a Saturday night. None of that mattered to me – I was going to have my own radio show.

I worked part-time at the college gym and purchased most of the records myself for the radio show. With my friend "Tone Def Jeff" Jones, we hosted the Contemporary Soul Show on WPRB for three consecutive years, giving the station some of its highest Arbitron ratings ever. We had listeners from all over the central New Jersey area, including Trenton, Camden, and New Brunswick. We even had loyal listeners from local correctional facilities. Over the years we were on the air, we received a steady influx of letters and calls from inmates who wanted to dedicate music to their loved ones. They would call from within the walls of Trenton State Prison, reaching us by any means necessary.

"This is AT&T with a collect call from Luther Vandross," the operator would blandly state. At which point the inmate would interrupt, screaming "Play 'Superstar!' Play 'Superstar'!'" By the time the operator realized that Luther Vandross was not the name of the caller, but the artist they were requesting, it was already too late. We knew that he wanted to hear "Superstar," and we would play it for him. Nothing gave us more pleasure than playing songs on behalf of inmates to their loved ones in the community. Being their voices to pass on their feelings through the songs they wanted was a powerful thing, and a privilege we didn't take lightly. We also invited New Jersey hip-hop artists to come battle on air, local DJs to do featured sets of hip-hop or house, and we played demos of unsigned vocalists for a listening audience who otherwise wouldn't have been exposed to their talent. We played music for a community in the central New Jersey area that didn't have many options for R&B formatted programming. Most of the college shows played Alternative Rock, and we felt like we were filling a glaring gap in the formatting of Princeton's radio station.

When Dad heard that being a radio DJ of hip-hop and R&B was my main extracurricular activity in college, I knew he wasn't pleased. He often questioned me on what use I would have for all those records once I got out into the real world. And secretly, my mother told me years later that both of them were extremely nervous that I would actually pursue deejaying as a professional career. To add insult to injury, a group of us formed a DJ group on campus. We called ourselves "FOPO" DJs and performed at local gigs in and around Princeton's campus. We brought house and hip-hop to a college nightlife culture that desperately needed an alternative to the abundance of beer kegs and rock music that plagued our campus during the late 1980s.

When my parents and sister came to my graduation in 1990, one of the biggest arguments I had with Dad was over a worn down table I had found at a garage sale on which I put my turntables and mixer. He didn't want me to put it in my car, said it looked cheap and dirty, and felt that once I left Princeton this "DJ thing" would be over. We argued about it incessantly outside of my dorm room while packing the car after the graduation ceremony, on a day that should have been free of any conflict and arguments. He was adamant that the cheap, dirty table on which I placed my turntables had no place in my car. Of course my tethered platform of bountiful character ended up being featured prominently in my car, and I kept it for years just to spite him. It wasn't until much later when compact discs became the primary music format and vinyl a rare commodity that he finally acknowledged their potential worth as collectibles. Long after my graduation, I remember him asking me, "Did you hold on to those records you used during college? They may be worth something now you know." I didn't know that vinyl would go out of style and be worth something later, but it felt good to have a renowned expert on antiques, watches, and clocks recognize the value in my own personal hobby. He never apologized for making such a scene about it on my graduation day, but him asking if I held onto them was about as close to an apology as I would get. So I accepted it.

After graduation, I traveled to East Lansing, Michigan to participate in a minority summer program at Michigan State University's College of Human Medicine to prepare for the Medical College Admissions Test (MCAT). My previous experience of tanking the PSAT in high school obviously didn't stick with me. I had a lackadaisical showing on my first MCAT, and realized I had to focus my efforts and study harder if I were to have a shot of getting into a good medical school. After the program ended, I returned home in August and spent some time with my parents before retaking the test in September. It was 1990 and Michelle was attending law school in California, so I was alone with them until I could take the test. The United States was about to invade Kuwait, George H. Bush was president, and my biggest concerns were what to do after the MCAT and getting my wisdom teeth pulled out.

I completed the MCAT and my wisdom teeth were removed by a local dentist without incident. Not long after I started to get the itch to leave Schenectady again. Being twenty-one, I just didn't feel it was cool to be living at home with my parents anymore, especially after getting a taste of the pseudo-independence that college life had afforded me. There were several cities I felt would've been good for me at the time, but Chicago rose to the top of the list. A good friend of mine from high school, Diana Sciocchetti, had moved there to live with her sister, and she told me I could stay with them until I found my own place. I didn't know how my parents would respond to me wanting to move to Chicago, but I could sense they were disappointed that I wasn't already in medical school. They wanted me to go out and do something with my life but also wanted me to be around them because they missed their son. It was a Catch-22 and whatever path I chose, it was likely they weren't going to be happy.

On a standard evening in October 1990, I sat down with my parents in the living room after dinner. The television was on, as it typically was, muttering gibberish and watching us pursue our individual interests. Mom was fastidiously going through bills and coupons while Dad was playing Dr. Mario on his Nintendo Gameboy. I sat reclined in my chair, seething in the perceived inconvenience of being young and wallowing in deferred independence. I brought up the topic of my potential move to Chicago, explaining that I needed to be out on my own and get some job experience while I applied to medical school. In my mind, I had it all figured out. I would go to Chicago, work as an orderly (medical assistant) in a hospital for a year, then enter whatever medical school accepted me in the fall of 1991. It was foolproof, except for the financial question of how I would get the money to move to Chicago. Of course, that was where my parents would come in. Most of my working experience was in college, and I hadn't saved a dime. I needed their help.

I explained to them that I would probably "only" need about $800-900 to take a bus or train out there and secure a place to live until I found a job. While I knew that was a lot of money, for some reason I was assuming that money really did grow on trees in the Malebranche house, despite my mother's insistence that it didn't. At that age, I truly didn't appreciate the blessing it was to have hard working parents who provided for me. So to my surprise, their answer to my financial request was an emphatic "No." They didn't feel they owed me an explanation, and they offered no alternative plans beyond me staying in upstate New York with them and watching my youth pass me by. Dad was dismissive in his summation of their decision, and never once lifted his gaze from his Nintendo Gameboy.

"David, we are not going to give you money to move to Chicago, and that is final," he muttered.

I was humiliated and furious. My father, the man who was a successful local surgeon, spent thousands of dollars on antiques I didn't think he needed, always flew first class on airlines when traveling to conferences, and had bought my sister a brand new car when she went to college wasn't willing to help me get started on a move to Chicago. I have never considered myself spoiled by any stretch of the imagination and I never asked for much from my parents in terms of handouts or money. So from my perspective, their refusal to help me move to get my life started was simply irrational and counterproductive to my development into adulthood. I decided that, at the wise age of twenty-one, I was going to speak my mind on this matter. I wasn't going down without a fight, so I came out swinging.

"Dad it's really amazing to me that you can shell out a thousand dollars with no problem when it comes to flying first class, but when it comes to helping your son become a man, you suddenly don't have any money," I cajoled.

"Ha!" I proudly thought to myself as I was consciously exerting my manly independence – that'll show him!

My self-congratulatory moment was short-lived, replaced by a surreal out-of-body experience. I was now hovering overhead, looking down at myself suffering from diarrhea of the mouth and wondering, "What the hell am I saying?" It was like watching a shaky figure skater perform at the Olympics. You know it's gonna turn out bad when she tries to do that triple axel but you just can't look away. But this wasn't Nancy Kerrigan or Tonya Harding, this was me and my father. The fall surely wasn't gonna be pretty. My suspicions were confirmed when Dad immediately shut off his Nintendo Gameboy. For the record, he *never* shut off his Gameboy until he decided he was done playing.

"What did you say?" He growled.

Before I knew it we were both screaming at each other. Suddenly he rose up and rushed over to my chair where I was sitting, reclined with my feet up. I had never seen him that angry before when he put his hands on the foot rest of my chair and started the motion of violently flipping me over, chair and all. But in the middle of his motion, he stopped himself and slowly tipped the chair over on its end so that it did not completely toss me on my back. Even when furious with me, he could not bring himself to hurt his son.

"If you don't like the rules here, you can get out of my house!" he bellowed as I scrambled off the overturned recliner and stood upright to face him.

The altercation happened so fast, and my mother was hysterical, crying and pleading for both of us to calm down. I went upstairs to my bedroom and began dramatically throwing clothes in my suitcase like a scene from some overacted Tyler Perry movie. Moments later, I came downstairs to see my father silently sitting again in his chair, and my mother crying, begging me not to go. I brushed by her and got the keys to *my* car, or the car Mom passed down to me for my last two years of college. Before I could put the luggage in the trunk, he came running out of the house and took the keys from me.

"If you think you are leaving here and taking your mother's car, you are sorely mistaken young man!" he shouted.

Dad was pulling rank on me, making me face the reality that at twenty-one years old, I didn't have the money, power, or influence to be able to move out on my own. Unfortunately, as much as I wanted to fight him on this point, he was right. I had a couple of credit cards but I would be leaving New York without much to my name and trying to start my life anew. Without any money to start off with, or their help, I was sunk.

Not wanting to concede defeat, I did what every red-blooded, young American who wants to get out of their parents' house does, I just left. I took my suitcase and wheeled it about two miles to the local Greyhound station in the middle of that chilly, autumn night. My parents didn't stop me, so I just kept going. About halfway there, I knew there was no going back, and I didn't care much if they tried to stop me or not. All I knew was that I didn't want to stay in Schenectady, or with them, any longer.

I got to the bus station late that night. It was closed until 5 a.m. I nestled myself in the empty inside hallway between the inner and outer glass doors, and slept on the hard tile floor with my suitcase by my side. It was a fitful sleep. I hadn't told them where I was going and it was cold. I dozed on and off wondering if they were looking for me, or if they were concerned that I was gone. Part of me didn't care. While I loved my parents dearly, it was time for me to go and become a man. If they weren't gonna help, I was determined to find a way to do it all by myself.

Five o'clock crept up slowly, so I gathered my belongings and stood outside, waiting for the first Greyhound employees to arrive. I got in line with the other early-rising customers and saw that the first bus to Chicago was leaving at 6 a.m. My plan was to hop on this bus and be in Chicago by the next day, ready to begin a new chapter in my life. Diana would come pick me up with her sister, I'd have a temporary place to live, and I could eventually get a job and get on with my life. As I approached the ticket counter to purchase my liberation papers, I reached into my pocket and realized that I didn't have my wallet with me. No wallet. No ID. No credit cards. No way would I be leaving upstate New York that morning. I frantically searched my bags and coat to no avail. I had left my wallet at the house and had no way to get to Chicago.

Dejected, I dragged my raggedy suitcase, now laden with misguided rebellion and misplaced pride, back up to my parents' house. When I arrived at the back porch, my mother was sitting at the kitchen table waiting for me. The same porch and table where tears of love, promise, and hope had flowed just four years earlier when I left for college. I would be leaving again, but this wasn't a mutually agreed-upon decision. She came quickly to the door with tears in her eyes. For as long as I've been alive my mother has been an anxious person, and I knew she hadn't slept at all not knowing where I was. But I was done fighting. I wanted to go and I was focused on the fact that I only came back to get my wallet and more personal belongings so I could be on the next bus to Chicago.

"David, where have you been?" She stammered. "We've been worried about you! Your father hasn't slept all night. He's been crying and sobbing. You're not going, are you?"

"I was at the bus station overnight. I came back to get my wallet. I left it in my room," I said coldly.

She grabbed and hugged me closely. I knew she understood my frustration but I also knew she wanted me to stay. I went up to my room, found my wallet, and sat on the bed to put some more things in my suitcase that I had forgotten in my rush to get out of the house earlier. A couple of minutes went by before I heard a knock on my door. It was my father. His hair was uncombed and the bags under his eyes moaned with fatigue. I had never seen him looking that disheveled.

"Son, can we talk?" he asked.

"Sure" I replied, though truly not interested in anything he had to say.

He sat on the bed next to me and put his hand on my knee. He was crying.

"You'll never understand what this feels like until you have kids of your own. You raise children, and they depend on you for everything. You watch them mature and become less reliant on you, and when they are all grown up - all they want to do is leave you. You'll never understand how much that hurts until you go through it yourself."

As Dad tearfully explained himself to me, I finally understood. He was giving me such a hard time and refusing to help me financially because he really wanted me to stay there with him and my mother. He just didn't know how to say it. In the blink of an eye, time had passed him by. All the missed football games, basketball games, and track meets, all the missed opportunities for father-son bonding as I was growing up flashed through his mind as I mentioned moving to Chicago. The memories he cherished, and those disrupted because he was tirelessly working to provide for his family, were carelessly dissipating in the air before his weary eyes. Now, more than ever, he just wanted to spend time with me, even if that meant not supporting me in my efforts to be independent and begin the transition to becoming a responsible adult. Even if it contradicted everything he taught me and raised me to be, he didn't want me to go. It all made sense now, and I didn't see him as a cold, robotic machine whose sole purpose was to make my life difficult anymore. He was my father, the man who had dedicated his life to nurturing me and getting me prepared to leave the nest and fly on my own. This same man was now having understandable second thoughts about the resounding finality of that moment. It signaled the end of my childhood but perhaps more importantly, it signaled the end of what he perceived would be his utility in my life as my father.

Standing on His Shoulders

We wept together, both of us mourning the reality of this occasion where father and son would most certainly part ways. The nature of our future relationship was staring directly into an all too certain alternative direction than that to which we were both accustomed. I knew we would be ok after that conversation, but I also knew it was time for me to leave and be on my own. I explained to him that I needed to gain some experience working, to actually go out and live in a world that was waiting for me. I needed to experience life outside of Schenectady with its big hair and incessant Bon Jovi songs blaring from every automobile. Life was more than keg parties and street races in souped-up cars on weekend nights. He understood my point even if he didn't necessarily agree with it, and we both gained some mutual respect for one another that morning. The same drive, work ethic, and stubbornness that brought him to the United States to become a successful surgeon, he was witnessing first hand in the mannerisms of his youngest son.

After more discussion, my parents decided to pull some money together for me. We drove together to the station, and I took a bus later that morning bound for Chicago. I can't imagine how hard that decision was for both of them. As I sat on that rickety bus, watching the blur of crimson and tangerine tree leaves pass my weary eyes, I could not help but think of how blessed I was to have the parents that I did. Dad always told me that he and Mom worked so hard when I was young because they wanted Michelle and me to stand on their shoulders and see further than they ever would. Dreaming of a brighter future for your children in America sometimes means that there will come that painful, paradoxical time. A time when those very children you have selflessly raised will want to leave and fly on their own to attain that very future you envisioned and for which you worked so hard. A future that, in my parents' hearts, they knew they can never have for themselves. In 1990, that time had come for me.

Loved ones will tell you how they feel, but not always verbally. Sometimes it comes out negatively. Sometimes it comes across as loving. Sometimes it appears that the motivation is malicious or evil. And sometimes you will never know what the underlying reasons are or why a loved one may act the way they do. For Dad, his reluctance to help me move to a new city to be on my own at the age of twenty-one was merely a reflection of his love for me. He didn't want me to leave. He didn't want things to change. He wanted me to stay around and continue to live with him and my mother. He wanted us to grow and experience life together as father and son. He wanted to forever be the Dad I relied on, laughed and joked with, learned from, and eventually grew to appreciate more up close. He wanted to make up for those lost moments in my life he had missed while he was focused on being a good provider. He just wanted more time.

9

Donna, Is Our Son Trying to Tell Us Something?

The Malebranche family didn't openly discuss sex or sexuality. There was never a wholesome Hallmark moment where either Mom or Dad sat down with me to say, "David, let's talk about the birds and the bees." It wasn't that they were trying to avoid it or deprive me of that education, but I think they both had trouble navigating that topic, as many parents do. By default, I had to learn about sex through the most reliable sources on the planet - my good friends, Playboy magazines, and porn. It was through these renowned experts that I learned several sexual "pearls of wisdom" that were helpful even though I wasn't even remotely having anything close to sex at the time. One of these truisms came from John Young, a dear, high school friend who unsuccessfully tried his best not to laugh at me when I told him that sex was when you peed inside a woman to make a baby. He explained that when you have sex with a woman, you don't actually *pee* in her to make a baby. He told me there's a funny white substance that comes out of you, goes into her, and when *that* happens, then you make a baby. I was astounded. Yup, I was the clueless kid everyone used to make fun of because I didn't have the vaguest idea about what to do with a girl.

What my classmates didn't know was that I wasn't really trying to have sex with girls in the first place – so their ribbing rarely caused me stress. I have been aware of my physical, emotional, and psychological attraction to other men from a very young age, probably as early as my pre-teen years. I can't explain it, I'm not interested in rationalizing it to others who don't understand it, and I don't have the patience to tolerate anyone who doesn't approve of it. All I know is that it's been a natural part of me for as long as I can remember. From having poorly understood male crushes on grade school friends and teachers to finding myself immensely attracted to male professional athletes and entertainers, I knew I was different from most. I was born this way.

I didn't act on this attraction until I started college. I was woefully behind the sexual activity curve in high school, primarily because my disciplinarian parents kept me on 11 p.m. curfew for the entire four years. Most of my classmates were already having sex in some way, shape, or form, but not me. I was so caught up in turning my grades from 97s to 100s, I didn't have time to think about sex. When I did experience intimacy, it was relegated to misguided fumblings with girlfriends, barely making it to second base in the back seats of cars and on weathered living room couches. In retrospect, these experiences and the turtle-like pace in which they developed were less reflective of the strict upbringing of my parents, and more about my general apathy towards women as romantic interests. My parents would not easily digest the knowledge of my bubbling attraction to men, so I figured it would be best for all parties involved if I just stuck to what I knew best: school and sports.

Being one of only two Black men in my class of over one hundred students, I didn't get much romantic attention from most of the White girls. I did make a connection with one of the two Black girls in my class, Monica O'Neal, and that was just fine with me. She was insanely beautiful and intelligent, reminiscent of a younger, more refined version of Ola Ray, the gorgeous model who played Michael Jackson's date in his *Thriller* video. Monica and I dated the typical way most kids do by going to proms, New Year's Eve parties, movies, and having dramatic breakups and arguments. Through our journeys, I always felt like something was missing. I could go through the motions, thinking I knew exactly how I was supposed to act with her, anticipating what a good boyfriend would do or say in certain situations. The passion was missing in our connection however, and physicality between us fizzled out far earlier than either of us expected. If you had asked me back then to identify what lead to our break up, I could admit to myself that it was because I was attracted to men, but I wasn't ready to claim that attraction as my own yet. It wasn't until I had my first sexual experience at eighteen with an older man from Barbados that I realized this was neither a choice nor a passing phase.

I spent the summer after my freshman year at Princeton working as a janitor in Ellis Hospital, the very hallowed halls in which my mother and father met over twenty years earlier. I worked partly to make money and partly because Dad would be there. I thought it would provide me with a chance to see him in action, and physically spend time in the environment that always kept him from spending time with sister, my mother, and me. As it turned out, with me cleaning rooms and Dad doing surgery, I rarely saw him at all. Someone I did see all the time was this Bajan man who worked at the hospital whom I will call "Andre." He was a short, unassuming brother, deep cocoa complexion who wouldn't make many stop to look twice when passing him. He wasn't handsome, but carried himself with a charisma and flair that took him far in his romantic pursuits. The first time I encountered him I was entering the hospital cafeteria. He caught my eye and waved furiously at me like we were long lost friends. I cautiously approached him in the food line.

"How are you brother?" he said in a carnivorous manner that flew over my head and bypassed any radar indicating that he was flirting with me. I paused, slightly confused by this new-found experience of how friendly folks in a hospital can be.

"I'm… fine. How are you?" I replied.

"I'm doing well man, doing well. It's *so* good to see you!" He shook my hand vigorously and held it just long enough to make the moment awkward.

"Uhhh… great!" I responded, trying my best to feign some semblance of recognition of who the hell this man was. He had a thick Caribbean accent and I concluded that maybe he knew my father through some fantastical West Indian connection. I let go of his hand as he walked away.

"I'll see you later brother!" Andre's pearly white teeth gleamed a little too brightly for someone who didn't know me. Yeah, I concluded, he must know my father. That's the only reason he's speaking to me.

"Great," I yelled back. "See you soon!"

I watched him walk away and went to get my food. On my way to eat with my co-workers, I passed Andre's table. As he saw me, he immediately stopped eating and grabbed my arm tightly as the others in his company looked at him curiously.

"You have to come see my place. I have so much to show you!" he said excitedly. I quickly became aroused by Andre's touch and walked away as if I had someplace to go. Being only eighteen at the time, I had not the slightest clue that when someone who doesn't know you gases your head up it usually means they're trying to get in your pants. My body sensed it, but my mind and logic failed to keep up. Welcome to the David Malebranche channel – featuring the sad and disconnected existence of a teenage virgin.

I spent the remainder of my workday cleaning my assigned areas of the hospital, desperately trying to avoid Andre while simultaneously wishing I could see him again. I longed to understand why his touch excited me in a way that the touch of my girlfriends' hadn't. Fifteen minutes before my shift was going to end, I ran into him while mopping a desolate hallway in the basement of the hospital. My heart raced excitedly.

"Well, hello again!" he exclaimed. I now fully understood what was happening, and how it was not coincidental that I was seeing him again. After some superficial talk, he invited me to join him for dinner the next week. He would cook steak, rent a couple of movies, and we could talk. Although something felt odd about the whole exchange, I was profoundly intrigued on a level I hadn't experienced before. So I said yes. He set a day and time, as I was clueless that this was actually a date and I was being courted like a school girl to a prom. My head was swirling with the types of lies I could tell my parents so I could investigate this strange man who had piqued my sexual and romantic curiosity. I told them I would be going over to a friend's house to watch movies, and left with Andre's address in hand. In 1987 there were no smartphones or GPS devices, and Google maps didn't exist. So I just did it old school – with the address and a map. Unfortunately, the street address Andre gave me had a name with duplicate locations in the area, so I spent the better part of an hour trying to find his place unsuccessfully. Finally, after feeling like a world class moron who couldn't find a simple address, I returned home. My parents had no idea what had just happened, oblivious to my true motivations behind getting out of the house that evening.

I didn't see Andre in the hospital for a couple weeks after our failed date night, and I was ok with that. My curiosity was dwarfed by my feelings of terror over what my attraction to men really meant. The next time I ran into him was on a day I wasn't scheduled to work, but had stopped by the hospital to pick up my paycheck. I was returning to my car, and he suddenly rushed up when he saw me, his face painted with hurt and disappointment from us not meeting.

"Hey, you stood me up that night! I had rented a VCR and movies, cooked steaks, and you just didn't show up. What happened?" he asked.

He wasn't bullshitting. Andre had truly put a lot of things together so we could meet, but all was forgiven now that I was standing in front of him.

"Yeah, the address you gave me I thought was another street, and I got lost." I told him. "Drove around for about an hour, but it wasn't getting me anywhere, so I just went back home. I thought maybe you had just given me the wrong address on purpose."

I put it back on him to mask my own sense of inadequacy for ruining our date.

"That's ok man, I understand. Hey, what are you doing now?"

"Going home."

"Can I get a ride? I took the bus up here to pick up my check and need to get back."

"Sure," I said hesitantly, not nimble enough to sidestep his ambush, and not yet fully understanding that his intentions of having me take him home were beyond just dropping him off.

I drove Andre back to his apartment that wasn't too far from where our house was. My mind was racing as he babbled on and on in the car. Were men like him all around me growing up and I just didn't see it? I hoped he wouldn't ask me the question when we arrived at his place, but he did.

"You wanna come up?"

I knew what my answer was before my lips could part to speak.

"OK."

We went up to his second floor apartment: a peculiar, old-fashioned one-bedroom living arrangement with archaic furniture that made you feel dusty just by looking at it. There were antique clocks, Hummel figurines, and even bowls of rock candy on a coffee table that only a grandmother could appreciate. We sat down facing each other on opposing couches and I nervously repositioned my flimsy red and black Adidas sweatpants so that he couldn't see I was already becoming aroused.

"You want some Kool-Aid?" he asked.

He was trying to dilute his sexual agenda in Kool-Aid? I was eighteen years old and didn't really care, as long as it was red Kool-Aid. If he had any other flavor I was out of there.

"Yeah, that would be great," I lied.

Not long after Andre hopped up and went to the kitchen, the doorbell rang. He came running out with a sparkling tumbler of red Kool-Aid filled to the rim, but suddenly looked nervous as he hastily handed me my cold beverage.

"Stay right there," he said, quickly exiting the living room.

I heard faint mumbling between him and another man by his front door. I couldn't make out what they were saying but it didn't sound like anything urgent. A couple of minutes passed and Andre made his way back in the living room.

"Who was that?" I asked inquisitively.

"My pastor from church. He was just coming to check up on me."

He seemed restless to move past the topic of his pastor, and I remember finding it strange that his pastor would be coming by to check up on him at the precise moment that I was there with him. He changed the subject quickly.

"So... are you curious?" he asked, leaning back on the couch.

"Curious? About what?" I said. I was good at feigning ignorance when I knew damn well what he was talking about.

"About me," he replied, his eyes narrowing in focus on me.

The antique clock on his wall ticked in a methodical way that gave me ample time to fully appreciate the life-changing moment currently propositioning me. I knew why I was there. He knew why I was there. Yet it seemed as if getting verbal consent from me would make his upcoming sexual encounter with a barely legal teenager morally permissible. Truth be told, I didn't care about his motivation. After eighteen years of a strict upbringing where I still didn't know what sex or physical intimacy felt like, I was ready to throw caution to the wind and be honest with myself about my sexual desires for the first time in my life.

"Yes," I replied.

The word lifted and flew into the sky like an emancipated bird, and no sooner had it released itself than Andre was hastily removing his clothes and trying to pull off mine. I can't imagine he actually enjoyed what transpired between us that humid summer afternoon. I don't recall whether I did or not, especially since I didn't know what the hell I was doing. What I do know is that the whole experience was over as quickly as it started and didn't involve intercourse. I hurriedly got dressed and drove home, where I laid on my bed and tried to forget what just happened - but I couldn't get it out of my head for weeks. I didn't see Andre much in the hospital after that, and when I did he acted as if nothing had happened, and even strangely disinterested. Maybe his pursuit of me was about the conquest, or maybe my sexual inexperience was just a big turn off. Either way, it took me almost a year before I had an experience with another man.

During the remainder of my college years, I basically retreated back into not being sexually active after that first experience with Andre. I continued to date women, and remember doing everything I could sexually with them, but never graduated to full intercourse. They turned me on, but I would be lying to myself if I said it felt as visceral an attraction that I had felt with Andre. By the time I started a sexual relationship with Marc Coleman, a friend with whom I used to DJ at Princeton, I was finally starting to digest the reasons behind my stunted sexual progress with women. I had girlfriends all my life but never felt a true emotional connection with them. It just felt different when I was with another man, and being with Marc felt natural. I didn't have to pretend I was enjoying what we were doing – I just did. Whether we were just hanging out or being physical, our relationship touched on every level of intimacy I could have experienced with another person. I thought to myself, "So this is how heterosexuals feel when they are with one another!" After discovering that another classmate Vince Smith was also "in the life," I was coming to the realization that there were other young Black men going through the same journey of sexual exploration that I was. My attraction to other men was not as unusual and unique as I had once thought.

In 1989, the summer between my junior and senior college years, I made my first pilgrimage to a Black gay club in New York City called Traxx. Until then, I had never realized how many Black same-gender-loving men existed in the world. Traxx was free on Tuesday nights, "welfare night" as the kids called it. Vince and I would take the New Jersey Transit train to Penn Station, go clubbing until six in the morning, and take the first train back to Princeton. The corporate drones who worked 9-to-5 would stare at us with judgmental eyes. They were envious of our youth and freedom, and we couldn't have cared less.

To say going to Traxx was a spiritual experience would be an understatement. My jaw dropped as I entered the hazy establishment, witnessing the undulating bodies of myriad beautiful Black and Latino men of all ages dancing in fellowship with a freedom I had never seen before. Everyone was vibrantly joyous and alive, without a care about the racial discrimination or sexual prejudice that would be waiting for us when the club closed and we resumed our everyday lives. Standing on the second floor of Traxx, I looked down upon an endless sea of glistening, gyrating figures. Every face was transfixed, gazing up to the heavens, arms lifted to the sky. Smoke lingered in the air long enough to provide alluring atmosphere, and the bass from the speakers shook the ground under your feet and the center of your soul. Alisha Myers sang "I Wanna Thank You" as if she was preaching the sermon that night, and her faithful congregants knew every word, fully embracing the song's resilient and appreciative message. In that moment, as a Black same-gender-loving man, I suddenly didn't feel so alone anymore. I was at home. That evening I also met the man with whom I would experience my first true relationship spanning four years. I was coming into my own and it felt good.

In 1991, by the time I entered Michigan State's College of Human Medicine in East Lansing, Michigan, I was pretty comfortable with my attraction to men. The year I had spent in Chicago after finishing college had served me well in this process. I got a chance to tell my good friend Diana about my attraction to men over a casual lunch. She was a little shocked, but did what any true confidant would do with that information – made sure that I was OK and just moved on. Chicago was also the setting where I was blessed to befriend some older Black same-gender-loving men in their thirties who didn't take advantage of me as a naïve twenty-one year old. These men taught and mentored me through stories of their lives and experiences. For that I was thankful. I was also fully in a love jones relationship with the young man I had met at Traxx in New York. We started a long distance relationship that connected his home in Atlanta with my nomadic journey from New Jersey to Chicago, and ultimately, Michigan.

It was as much of a relationship as you can have between two testosterone-heavy young men in their early twenties. There was passion, intimacy, compromise, and plenty of intense arguments. We struggled with how to handle our profound love for one another despite both of us being emotionally immature. It was my first crash course in how to navigate a same-sex relationship. I had no idea that a disagreement between us would be the proverbial springboard to my parents learning about my sexual orientation.

Our relationship was more often turbulent than not, and we both didn't know how to get off the ride. Life was happening all around us and we could do little to control it. His mother had died unexpectedly in 1992 in Atlanta and it became increasingly challenging to maintain our connection while he was dealing with that trauma. I was distracted and overwhelmed, failing classes in medical school at Michigan State and struggling just to stay afloat. I felt more isolated and alone than ever in my cold one-bedroom apartment in East Lansing. So while I was on my month break between my first and second years of medical school in August of 1992, I went home to spend some time with my parents in upstate New York. They had purchased a property in Galway that they planned to use as a summer getaway, reminiscent of the lake house we occupied in Sacandaga when I was a child. My visits home were restorative and rejuvenating to me – I could relax, enjoy Mom's home cooking, and recharge my battery for the upcoming school year. The only stress plaguing me was the building tension between my parents and me regarding my love life. I was quite certain they were now expecting me to bring girlfriends and potential wives home for their approval. Instead, I was struggling internally with how to delicately inform them that girls would not be part of my relationship future at all.

My decision on when and how to disclose my sexual orientation to my parents was excruciatingly difficult, but became unavoidable due to my impetuous nature as a young man. I didn't think things through back then, and diarrhea of the mouth was a common affliction from which I suffered. I rarely considered the future implications of words and actions. In the spirit of this reality, I made the mistake of having an argument with my boyfriend while I was on my parents' home phone. Our discussion was intense and emotional, leaving me drained when we finished. Not having much of a poker face, I left the living room visibly shaken. When I passed my mother on the outside porch, she immediately stopped me.

"What's wrong?" she said, looking very concerned and maternal, like she usually did.

I paused. I was exhausted, emotionally spent, and in that split second decided that I did not have the energy to lie to her.

"You really want to know?" I asked.

"Yes, I do." She obviously didn't realize what she was getting into when she said that, but I obliged anyway.

"I just had an argument with my boyfriend of three years. We're having a tough time right now," I admitted.

She paused, her face contorting as she examined me with disappointed eyes that began to well up with tears.

"I knew," she sighed.

Standing on His Shoulders

People always say mothers "know" when their sons are same-gender-loving, and Donna Malebranche was no exception. Her suspicion was confirmed when she opened up a package that had been mailed to their house while I was in school. The package contained promotional materials from a Black gay pornographic company in Los Angeles from whom I had previously purchased videos during college. The materials showed, in her shocked words, "Black men engaged in sexual acts with each other." She threw it away, thinking they had sent it to the wrong address – but she knew. She was just in denial as a lot of mothers are about their sons who don't pursue a heterosexual behavior pattern of dating and relationships. Any same-gender-loving man who has a close relationship with his mother can act like she doesn't know if he doesn't verbally tell her. But it is likely that she already does know, and is just waiting for him to initiate the conversation out of respect and not to make him feel uncomfortable. In this regard, Mom was no different from a million of her predecessors and the millions of mothers after her who will have similar experiences with their sons.

To her credit, she actually handled the whole situation relatively well, and we both decided that the best course of action would be to *not* tell my father. Old school West Indian fathers and same-gender-loving sons usually mix as well as oil and water. We could all avoid an explosive situation by just keeping quiet about this secret. So Donna Malebranche made a promise to not say a word about the subject. It was a promise she kept for an entire year. She never spoke of it when I was home and uttered not a word to my father about my intimate relationships. This was not difficult to do, as even when I had girlfriends in college, I kept them away from my parents because they always felt the girls were never good enough for me. So it was a logical extension to keep my sexual orientation a secret. If they wouldn't approve of any romantic partners from the socially acceptable female gender, approval of a male romantic interest, even if he was a Harvard graduate, was surely out of the question. So Dad remained in the dark about my romantic inclinations, no worse for the wear, until I met Darren Hathaway.

Darren was the last person you would think was a medical student, much less a future physician. He boasted luxuriously long auburn hair down past his shoulders, large hoop earrings in both ears, loose fitting clothes that looked like they were just yanked off a Salvation Army rack, and several ornate rings on his fingers. I remember being struck by how free and uninhibited he was. He wore whatever he wanted, sported whatever jewelry he chose, and didn't seem to care what anyone thought about it. If his attire crossed gender lines or blurred the lens through which others viewed his sexual orientation, so be it. To top it all off he was a White male, straight, and had a gorgeous Black girlfriend named Jackie. Together they made the cutest couple in the world, a modern day inverse re-imagining of my parents. I fell in love with them immediately.

Darren and I forged a strong friendship those first two years of medical school, and he was the one who convinced me to get my ear pierced at a local mall in Michigan. I chose my left ear because the unwritten rule back then was that, if you were a man, it was cool and heterosexual to have an earring in your left ear, but you were somehow boarding the train to Gayville if you pierced your right ear. Guys with earrings in both ears were somewhat of an enigma - a crapshoot as to whether people would perceive them as straight, gay, or maybe even bisexual. Of course these rules don't mean a damn thing in the real world, but for some they provide structure to their lives, especially when they need to quickly assess someone's sexuality based on a superficial trait. So when I traveled home during a break that first year of medical school with an earring in my left ear, Dad took notice.

"So, you got an earring, huh son?"

"Yeah, Dad, I did."

That was the extent of our earring conversation. He asked the question to let me know that he didn't approve, but I imagine at that point he was growing tired of trying to impose his will on his children. It would've taken too much energy out of him to make a fuss about it. So he just made mention of it and moved on, and I was truly thankful for that.

But when I decided to get an earring in my right ear during my second year of medical school, I wasn't prepared for the trajectory my journey with my father would take as a result. I don't know what inspired me to get the second earring, but I just felt it was time. Being the impulsive soul I always prided myself in being, I just did it. I drove home less than a week later to see my parents during summer vacation in August 1993. I was twenty-four years old. When I got there, things were business as usual in the Malebranche household. We talked about life, politics, sports, school, and my thoughts on my future in medicine.

When I consider that time of my young adulthood, I used to think I was pretty smart. So in preparation for my parents' certain traumatic reaction to me having two earrings instead of the one they had just grown accustomed to, I devised a plan. I concocted the brilliant, fool-proof idea to take the left earring out and just leave the right one in. It was an obvious choice - the right earring had to stay in so that the hole wouldn't close up. Besides, my parents weren't hip enough to pay attention to which ear the earring was in, right? Wrong. My first night home I was sitting on the living room floor watching TV. Dad was in his reliable rocking chair, Nintendo GameBoy in hand, when out of the blue he glanced down at me.

"Son, is that an earring in your right ear?" he asked.

I was shocked at the question. Was my Dad, the old school Haitian, trying to clock me?

"Yeah, Dad, it is." I said sheepishly. I was a little nervous as to where his question would lead us.

In an eerily déjà vu moment, he simply went right back to the GameBoy without another word. I couldn't help but think to myself how maybe Dad was mellowing out in his older age. I envisioned how the process of "inviting him in" when discussing my sexual orientation was going to be easier than I had originally thought. Mom glanced over at me and didn't say a word.

The next morning I woke up a little late, and came downstairs to the kitchen, where my mother was seated at the table. Dad had already left for the hospital. As I sat down, she didn't waste any time getting right to the point.

"David, I don't know what to tell your father. He's asking me questions," she said worriedly.

"What are you talking about?" I asked.

"Did you tell him last night that you got an earring in your right ear?"

"Yeah, he asked, so I told him yes. I took out the other one and thought he wouldn't notice, but he did."

"Well, he asked me this morning, he said 'Donna, is our son trying to tell us something?' And I didn't know what to say."

Whenever my Dad calls my mother by her first name to ask her a question or make a statement, it's usually something he considers important or wants to emphasize. If he was looking for a book he couldn't find and became increasingly exasperated, he would exclaim, "Donna, where's my book?" When she stepped on his foot by accident while walking by him one day when he was in a particularly bad mood, he exclaimed in an emphatically thicker Haitian accent, "Donna, that's my foot!" So the fact that he used her first name in asking what was up with me, told me he was serious about this earring thing. Despite being an old school West Indian man, apparently he was hip enough to equate a man having an earring in his right ear with a non-heterosexual lifestyle. I was at a loss for words for a solution to help my mother with this sudden conundrum.

"Mom, I don't know what you can say. Just don't tell him. He'll forget about it," I reassured her.

How wrong I was. Not only did my father *not* forget about my right earring, but he made it the staple of every morning conversation with my mother for the next few days as they had breakfast together before work. And each time, she would inform me that he had asked again. And again. And again. Finally, after three days of this broken record playing, I gave her an ultimatum, because I was sick of hearing about it.

"Mom, look, if he isn't man enough to ask me about this earring and what he thinks it means to my face, then he isn't man enough to get any kind of answer from me. Go ahead and tell him tomorrow morning when he asks. I really don't care anymore."

I didn't want Mom to be the go-between for this father-son lack of communication anymore. It was unfair to her, and I knew it was tearing her up inside. She had always played the role of emotional translator between Dad and me, but this situation in particular was stretching her thin. Even though she knew about my sexual orientation, she didn't like keeping secrets from her husband. So I just went ahead and gave her the green light. Beyoncé would have been proud.

The next morning when he asked during breakfast conversation, she told him. Later that day, when he was seeing patients in the office, Mom came out to prepare dinner like she usually did and caught me in the living room watching TV.

"Well, I told him," she shared.

"Really? What did he say?" I asked quizzically, as if I really thought there were varied options of how a sixty-year-old Haitian man would respond to finding out his son was same-gender-loving.

"He didn't say anything. I don't think he's pleased," she said woefully.

The next few days were pretty routine and uneventful, except for one small thing – my father didn't say a word to me or even acknowledge my presence in the house. He merely talked to my mother, went to the hospital to perform surgery, saw patients in the office, but he wouldn't even look at me. The ritualistic morning and evening kisses that were a constant reminder that he was present stopped as well. The tension in the air between us was so thick that I thought the house would explode at any moment.

My mother was in the middle of things for this whole unfolding of events, just as she had been when I left home for Chicago years earlier, but this father-son spat was lasting much longer than one night. She kept giving me minute-by-minute updates like a CNN correspondent on what my father was thinking and if he was ready to talk to me yet. This was obviously a tough pill for him to swallow. He would have to take some time to prepare himself to be able to discuss it with me face-to-face.

Dad finally decided to call a family discussion about my sexuality a couple of days before I was planning to drive back to Michigan to return to school. Almost a full week had gone by and he had sufficient time to mull it over and get his thoughts together. We would sit down to talk things out man-to-man. The air was sticky that night on Galway Lake, and crickets chirped outside as a rustic soundtrack to our conversation while we sat at the kitchen table. He and I, elder father and son in emerging adulthood, talked while my mother sat on the side trying her best to play the impartial referee. It was a bout of epic proportions.

My father spoke first with an honesty and frankness that I hadn't seen since the morning I left for Chicago years earlier. He told me about his life and dreams growing up in Haiti, as well as his hopes and aspirations for the life he wanted when he arrived in America. He spoke of the foundation he was laying, the countless hours he worked, his commitment to providing for our family, and the reason why he bought the property on Galway Lake in the first place. He wanted a space where he could sit back when he was retired. Dad had plans of securing a location where Michelle and I could come with our respective families and spend time there with them. Most importantly, he bought the property with the vision that Michelle and I would provide him with grandchildren, and this scenic camp would provide these grandchildren with a safe place to play when they were young. My attraction to other men was ruining this dream and his entire life as he knew it.

While Dad spoke, his voice was steady and firm. He seemed angry, but as I studied his face, I suddenly realized I was looking at a man who wasn't angry, but one who was grieving. Grieving the perceived loss of the dreams he had constructed for his son. Grieving over the realization that I wasn't going to ever be exactly how he wanted me to turn out. I explained to him that I wasn't doing this to him with the conscious intent of ruining the American dream for which he had worked so hard. I was simply being myself. While I was sorry about his disappointment over me not fitting into his well-laid life plans for my future, this was who I was, and it wasn't going to change.

The conversation got heated at moments, and at other times there was mutual understanding and respect. A lot of tears were shed and I saw my father cry for the fourth time in my life. The first time was when his father (Papa) passed away, the second when I left for Princeton, and the third the morning I left for Chicago. I was shaken and felt awful, almost guilty in some respects, but there was really nothing I could do. I knew that my true romantic and intimate interests were with other men, and this was not something I could conveniently turn on or off to appease the idealistic visions of my immigrant father. After there was nothing more to say, and the tacit conclusion for both of us was that we would have to agree to disagree, I decided to leave. I had a couple days left before I was to return for school, but I suddenly didn't feel comfortable at home anymore. I was overcome with the sense that despite all I had achieved up until that point, none of it would be good enough to make up for their negative view of my sexuality. I felt like a stranger in my own family. It was 11p.m., and I decided to pack my stuff and drive the twelve hours through New York and Canada to East Lansing. Driving has always been a form of therapy for me, as it affords me time to think, clear my head, and just have some time to myself. My car hastily transported me home that night, getting me back to my apartment around ten in the morning. When I finally laid my head down to sleep, I had one of the most restful periods of slumber I had had in years.

David J Malebranche

After our discussion, the topic of my attraction to other men didn't come up that often between my father and me. To this day it has never been the focal point of conversation between us like it was that fitful August night. Over time, he has come to realize that who I am romantically associated with does not fully define who I am. Similarly, I realized that he would never be capable of giving me relationship advice or helping me navigate how to date other men. We don't have typical father-son moments of discussion about my relationships. I've had to come to peace with how my father accepts this part of my life; very much in the same way he has had to come to peace with me being who I am. Perhaps the most important aspect of inviting my parents into my sexual orientation was not about them forgiving me for who I am, but rather about me forgiving them for being incapable of fully embracing that part of me.

Years later, during the winter of 2000, a full seven years after he found out about my sexuality, I experienced a watershed moment in understanding how far Dad had come with accepting me for who I am. While working as a Preventive Medicine resident at the New York City Department of Health, I was asked by a community-based organization in Albany to give a talk about health and wellness for a group of Black same-gender-loving men. I had been sharpening my oratory skills by giving public speeches to various groups, mostly on medical and public health topics. My practice was to identify my sexual orientation as part of the talk so that the audience would feel comfortable and know where I was coming from. I disclosed so that they realized the person who was giving them health information actually understood that part of their lived experience. But this speaking engagement was different. Albany is only ten or fifteen minutes from my birthplace of Schenectady. My father was one of the most well-known surgeons in the area. Most importantly, Malebranche certainly isn't the most common name. So I knew that if I came to speak for a community-based organization, people would put two and two together. My father could catch some flak based on me disclosing my sexual orientation during the talk.

I decided to be proactive and do some damage control. While relaxing in my Harlem apartment one night, I called Dad to tell him that I was coming to Albany to do a presentation, and inform him of my intention to disclose my sexual orientation as a part of the talk. I told him so that he would hear what I was doing from me, and not from some nosy gossiper in upstate New York who may try to use this information to hurt him in some way. I had too much respect for him, his journey to this country, his hard work as a surgeon, and his reputation in my birthplace to allow that to happen.

Dad didn't say a word during my canned speech. When I was finished, he paused and sighed before he spoke.

"Son, I've realized over the years that what I have thought was best for you and your life may not have been best for you, or what you wanted. I know that you are not a 'flaming queen' and I would not care if someone came to me from work and said something negative about you. You are my son and I love you."

I cried softly as he spoke. Seven years of not discussing my sexual orientation, and this was what he had to say. I wasn't crying out of disappointment or hurt, but over the simple fact that we could now have this conversation as father and son. Some may wonder why I would be moved to tears over Dad saying that he knew I wasn't a flaming queen. I think he expected that with the acknowledgment of my being attracted to men, I would immediately be transformed into a stereotypical, hyper-effeminate, "gay" caricature often portrayed in the media. This seemed to be one of my father's biggest fears - not so much around my attraction to men, but more about how this would affect my masculinity. Over the years, as he continued to interact with me and realized that I was still the same person I was before I disclosed my sexual orientation, it calmed his spirit.

While someone telling you that they know you are not a flaming queen is not using the phrase in a complimentary fashion, I realized at that moment that for my father, that was the best it was going to get. He may not ever say, "Son, I'm just elated that you love other men" or "Tell me all about your new boyfriend David," but his words were the closest version of a sentiment of acceptance and respect for which I had been longing for so many years. Whether he approved or disapproved, understood or didn't understand my sexual orientation, he was letting me know that he loved me regardless because I was his son. That was all that mattered, and everything I needed to hear.

It would have been unfair of me to engage him in an academic discussion of how offensive it was to describe effeminate men as flaming queens. That wasn't the point. This is the man who would have trouble telling me he was proud of me for getting a 97 grade point average or being elected to a committee making national HIV/AIDS policy decisions. Why would the same father who was brought up never to be satisfied with second place tell me he was proud of me for sharing what he considered a socially unacceptable sexual orientation? I had to change *my* expectations of him uncon-ditionally accepting or agreeing with every part of my life. I chose to be thankful that he was honestly expressing to me exactly how he felt, even if it was disapproval or tempered acceptance. Dad will always undeniably and unapologetically be who he is, which is fine with me, because I will continue to be who I am whether he accepts it or not. I love him for who he is, and I know he loves me for who I am. Like father, like son.

10

MAN OF STEEL

After the conversation about my sexuality, relating with Dad felt awkward and strained for a while. We were both in our own heads, replaying how we each felt and what we had said. We were holding private narratives on our own while not reaching across the aisle to invite the other to join the conversation. We still talked on the phone, still said our obligatory "I love yous" at the completion of our conversations, and still had our communal musings about race and politics when I came home. Our relationship, however, was undoubtedly different. There was a lot not being said, uncomfortable pregnant silences sitting between us, and an overall sense of two men tolerating their disagreement. It was like when you pass someone walking down the street every day for months, never stopping to say "hi." One day you decide to say "hi" and the person explodes into the biggest smile. He was thinking you didn't like him, while you were thinking the same. That's how Dad and I treated each other for a couple of years after we discussed my sexual orientation. We were passing each other while never bothering to say "hi."

Meanwhile, at medical school, since I had previously failed a few classes during the summer semester of 1992, I was fully engaged in the painstaking process of remediating those classes to get off academic probation. In the fall of 1993, I also began to look into transferring medical schools and moving to Atlanta. While I enjoyed Michigan State's College of Human Medicine as a school and was thankful for the education I was receiving, the Midwest as a cultural experience was killing me. Part of my reasoning for attending Michigan State was that East Lansing as a city was small and a bit off the beaten path. As a medical student, I knew I would have to focus on my studies. Living in a city that didn't have much of a social atmosphere and required an hour drive to get to Detroit for some nightlife would help me be a better student. I didn't anticipate being so stressed from school and frustrated with not having a decent social life that I would make that drive to Detroit as often as I could to find any distraction. My boyfriend also lived in Atlanta, and despite the ups and downs we had endured, I wanted to be wherever he was. Plus, being a young, Black man in the 1990s, Atlanta was considered the Black Mecca. I was excited about the possibility of participating in the raucous street celebration that was Freaknik, reveling in 70 degree warmth in December, and experiencing an environment where Black folk actually fixed their mouths to say hello in passing. Atlanta has always represented a place where ample employment and personal advancement opportunities for Black people is the norm. Whether the latter part of that statement is true or not is debatable, but for me it didn't matter. Moving to Atlanta meant a brighter future for both my career and social life.

In 1991, while living in Chicago, I applied to Emory University medical school in Atlanta, but was put on the waiting list. Upon hearing that news, I became so preoccupied with migrating to Atlanta that I drove south with the intentions of improving my status on the waiting list by talking directly to the Dean of Admissions. I was still together with my boyfriend at the time. He was working at a local hotel in Buckhead, so during a visit I used one of their pay phones to call the admissions office. I was excited that I could potentially help myself get into Emory's Medical School and finally move to Atlanta. My plan was to position myself as best I could on that waiting list, so my fingers were brimming with anticipation and hope as I dialed the phone.

"Admissions Office, can I help you?" The angelic voice of the administrative assistant greeted me on the phone.

"Hi, my name is David Malebranche," I started cordially. "I got a letter that I was waitlisted for the entering class of 1991. I'm here visiting from Chicago and was wondering if I could meet with the Dean sometime this week to discuss my application?" My tone was so syrupy pleasant and professional, I was certain they would bump me up on the waiting list just by hearing my voice alone.

"Hold on a second. Let me get your file," she said, placing me on hold.

My mind drifted to Piscean visions of getting a quick appointment with the Dean and him being overwhelmed by what a great candidate I was. After some frivolous banter he would lament over how the admissions committee could even consider waitlisting me. He would then admit me on the spot, thereby cementing my place in the incoming first year medical student class at Emory University. I cuddled with my dreams in that phone booth as blurred figures of busy people passed me by in the hotel. Patrons checked in and out and harried front desk clerks typed furiously on computer keyboards while I waited. After several moments, the assistant returned to the phone.

"Mr. Malebranche," she chirped.

"Yes," I replied, pulling out my scheduling calendar and pen in eager anticipation.

"There's been some kind of clerical error. According to your file you should've been rejected months ago."

I couldn't breathe.

"Are you sure?" I asked.

"Yes. Says right here you were rejected. You should have received a rejection letter in the mail. I'm awfully sorry for the misunderstanding. Have a nice day."

I wanted to rip the phone out of the wall. I came all the way down to Atlanta just to find out that I was rejected. Saying I was mortified would have been an understatement. I felt like a fool. Despite the bad news about Emory, I still kept the dream of returning there someday in my mind. Living in East Lansing made me realize that the Midwest was definitely not where I wanted to be. I rededicated myself to improving my school performance so I could apply for a transfer down to Atlanta, regardless of whether it was Emory, Morehouse, or the Medical College of Georgia in Augusta. The opportunity to do my clinical medical school years in a place where there were a lot more upwardly mobile Black people was becoming more appealing with every passing day, and represented the proverbial light at the end of the tunnel. I discovered a more efficient way of studying, sought help from other students and academic sources when I needed it, and spent endless hours in libraries and hospital conference rooms committing class work to memory. After remediating my previously failed classes and improving my current performance, I was taken off academic probation. That semester I sent my request for a transfer application package to Emory for their consideration.

In 1994, after our spring semester ended, I spent three weeks in Atlanta to participate in a board exam prep course that was being held at a local downtown hotel. I was never the best standardized test taker (as the SAT and MCAT exams had already proven), so I enrolled in the course to make sure I passed the exam. It was a grueling three weeks of daily 8 a.m. to 5 p.m. lectures and workshops on core material needed to pass the boards with only two days off. I attended these sessions with a focused vigor, and committed my evenings to reviewing the material presented each day. By the end of those three weeks, I knew I was ready. After finishing the exam and returning home to Michigan, the first message I retrieved on my answering machine was from the Emory University School of Medicine Admissions Office. They had accepted me for a transfer into the graduating class of 1996, contingent upon my passing of the board exam. Needless to say, I was excited. In July of 1994 I moved to Atlanta and began my clinical rotations at Grady Memorial Hospital. Life was good and it seemed like everything was falling into place. My academics were back on track, I had successfully transferred to Emory, and in less than two years I would be a physician. Not long after, I was notified that I had passed the board exam. I couldn't remember a time when I was happier with my professional life.

That winter, after moving to Atlanta, I went home like I usually do for Christmas vacation. I flew this time, avoiding the fifteen hour drive back and forth through the predictable northeast cold and snow. When I arrived at the Albany airport, my mother was waiting for me, her face despondent and sorrowful. As I approached her, I suddenly realized that Dad wasn't with her as he always was for my return visits home.

"Where's Dad?" I said.

"Your father's not feeling well, so I just came to get you myself." she replied.

"What's wrong? Is he OK?"

"He's OK, he's just a little under the weather and has been fighting a cold that just hasn't gone away."

The drive home that night felt a little longer than usual. Mom was deathly quiet, and sadness lingered in the air like an uninvited guest. My father, the tireless surgeon, the man to whom I would always look for energy and strength, my own personal Superman, was not feeling well enough to even come to the airport to meet me. It felt strange. I knew he had high blood pressure but that runs in our family. I also knew that he had a low white blood cell count, which is relatively common in people of African descent. I had never really heard or seen him feeling so bad physically that he couldn't meet me at the airport. Dad was like the postal service when it came to being a doctor and seeing his family – nothing could keep him from it. Certainly a minor head cold couldn't knock him out, could it?

The house was as quiet as a funeral parlor as my mother and I approached it. The back kitchen door squeaked in pain as we made our way inside to an eerie ambiance I had never experienced there. I walked through the kitchen and into the hallway that led to our family room. My father sat in his familiar rocking chair, covered to his neck in an old blanket. His eyes were closed, hands dangling off the armrests of his chair, and he was barely moving. His entire demeanor was that of an 80-year-old nursing home resident, not a 62-year-old practicing surgeon.

"Hi Dad," I said quietly, careful not to arouse him too suddenly.

He slowly opened his glazed eyes and turned his head towards me. I kissed him on the forehead.

"Oh, hi son, how are you?" he said weakly.

"I'm good Dad. I just got in. Mom said you weren't feeling too well."

"Oh, it's just a little cold I'm having trouble getting over."

"OK. I'm just gonna get my stuff unpacked upstairs and get settled. I'll be back down in a minute."

He closed his eyes again, and I walked back into the kitchen in tears. Mom could look at me and tell that I was shaken by how he looked. It didn't appear serious enough that he needed to be hospitalized, but it was definitely a wakeup call regarding the humanity and vulnerability of the man I once considered invincible. As I went upstairs and unpacked my clothes, I began to think about the timing of this mysterious illness he was suffering from, and why he couldn't get over this as quickly as he normally did in the past. Sure, one could pass it off as old age and the progressive weakening of his immune system, but he wasn't that old. He was only in his early 60s and it didn't make sense to me why now he would be appearing and reacting to illness like this.

But it made perfect sense. In the past year, Dad had learned about my sexual orientation and he was disapproving of Michelle's current boyfriend, whom he felt was beneath her. His surgical practice was bustling with patients, and he had recently employed another young surgeon to help him out with his suffocating caseload. Overworked professionally and unhappy personally, he appeared dissatisfied with where his life was going at the moment. The majority of this malcontent stemmed from abject disappointment with his children's personal lives, despite how Michelle had recently graduated from law school, and I would soon obtain my medical degree. It seemed that her poor selection of boyfriends, and the fact that I would want boyfriends at all, was taking a toll on him physically. That Christmas, my father was dealing with a lot I was aware of, and probably a whole lot I wasn't. His body was under duress due to issues over which he had little control, and it wasn't responding well.

Christmas came and went that year, and Dad seemed to physically improve just by having Michelle and me home for the holidays. The positive aspects of having his children around, however, were short-lived as Michelle journeyed back to California, and I to Atlanta to continue the slavery called clinical medical school rotations. Long, arduous hours, few days off, taking certification exams, and doing grunt work for senior residents and physicians was the typical life of a third year medical student. On the cusp of establishing my own career, my relationship with Dad was coming to a cross-roads. We weren't talking much, and he seemed more distant than ever before, both geographically and emotionally. Mom would inform me that on his medical checks, his white blood cell count was still low, and he was having some abnormalities with his liver tests as well. Of course he would downplay this when I tried to bring up the subject with him, but she was concerned. I always trusted her as my father's emotional translator, so I believed her narrative on his condition.

It had been well over a year since we had our discussion about my sexual orientation, and not only had the quality of our interactions deteriorated, but the quality of his health was insidiously declining as well. I convinced myself that somehow this was my fault. It seemed that no matter how successful I was in life, Dad's disappointment over my poor fit into his heterosexual American dream would always taint me as a failure in his eyes. For a Haitian father with a same-gender-loving son, this was a fate worse than death. Outside of changing the essence of who I was, there was nothing I thought I could do. Then I recalled my good friend from grade school, Bill Brazell. Bill was the first classmate I remember befriending in first grade at St. Helen's elementary school in Schenectady. He taught me how to take a plastic sandwich bag, blow it up and pop it to scare the hell outta anyone in the surrounding area. A tall, lanky White boy with a devilish grin and cereal bowl haircut, he was hands down the most intelligent kid in our class and one of the smartest people I have ever had the pleasure to know. We instantly became friends, and maintained the relationship through the varying milestones in our lives such as college, bad jobs, knucklehead girlfriends and boyfriends, his marriage, and the birth of his three, beautiful daughters. His tragic flaw lies in his affliction with liking the Boston Red Sox. Since I am a New York Yankees fan, it flew in the face of common logic that the two of us could sustain a meaningful friendship over the years. But that's exactly what we managed to do.

As a kid, I remember going to Bill's house to play games and hang out. His father was a brilliant, intimidating man with a booming bass voice and thick horn-rimmed glasses. I was scared shitless of him whenever I came by to visit, because I knew that despite just going there to play games, I would be subjected to myriad mental gymnastic exercises for which I was never adequately prepared. He would sit both of us down to participate in various hand-written math and brain quizzes to test our knowledge and intellectual acumen. No matter how bright I thought I was walking into Bill's house, I would always leave feeling like a moron. I knew that Bill's father had a tremendous amount of respect for Dad and me. It was actually an honor that he would want to engage me, because he didn't see all of our classmates as being on Bill's intellectual level. Participating in these games, however, would often compound the already lingering sense of inadequacy my father had imprinted in my psyche.

When the time came for us to go to high school, Bill's father came by the house and talked with Dad about enrolling me at Portsmouth Abbey School in Rhode Island. Portsmouth Abbey was a prep school that Bill's great uncle, a generous man of the cloth, had offered to pay his tuition, room and board. Bill's father felt that he and I were gifted students, and investing in our high school education at Portsmouth Abbey would best serve us for the future. He also understood how close Bill and I had become over the years as friends. His concern was that this friendship would suffer as a result of Bill leaving to attend this New England school if I chose to stay in Schenectady. Dad agreed but, along with my mother, thought it best to leave the decision to me. Attending a prep school in another city would mean severing ties with a lot of the friends I had made over the years. Even if it meant my friendship with Bill could suffer, maintaining several others by staying at the local Catholic high school would probably be less traumatic to me. My parents also did not like the idea of me leaving home so soon and they wanted to keep me near them for as long as they could before college. They left the decision with me, but in many ways it was still theirs to make. So I stayed put.

Standing on His Shoulders

Bill and I parted ways for our respective high school educations, me staying in Schenectady and him moving to Rhode Island. Our friendship suffered, as we didn't speak as frequently as we had in grade school, but we still did keep in touch. During the summer of 1984, between my sophomore and junior years in high school, I came down to have breakfast like any other day. My mother, looking solemn, showed me the newspaper's local news section. Bill's father was missing after an accident in which the currents in the local river caused his fishing boat to capsize. Bill's two sisters, both swim team members, were able to emerge from the water unscathed, but the current was so strong that it pulled his father down instantly.

A group of us gathered at Bill's house to check on him and pay our respects to his father. It was difficult to see him – gone was the infectious grin and jovial, quick-witted nature that was always part of his personality. In its place was a somber, long-faced, vacant shell of the friend I knew and loved. We attended the wake and funeral but I never got to speak with Bill one-on-one due to him being the oldest male in the family. He was thrown into the role of substitute father for the day, unable to carve out the mental and physical space to grieve the terrible loss he had just suffered. The whole situation shook me to my core. I couldn't help but think about how it would have affected me at that point in my life if Dad had been unexpectedly taken away from me.

Years went by, and Bill and I kept in touch sporadically. His education and work took him though Boston, California, and New Mexico, while my journey carried me through New Jersey, Michigan, Chicago, and Atlanta. We always seemed to gravitate back to one another no matter how much time had lapsed between conversations or relocations. He was and will always be one of my closest friends whose impact in my life is measured in quality, not quantity. After not talking for years, we could pick up the phone and reconnect as if no time had passed at all.

One of these serendipitous moments of reconnection came around the same time I was struggling to maintain some semblance of a healthy relationship with my father in 1995. A couple of years had passed since Dad had learned of my sexual orientation, and things were still rocky between us. I told Bill about the issues we were having, and asked for his advice. He opened up and told me about his relationship with his father before he died, including the severe ups and downs he had with him during grade school. This was the same time I was starting to have some growing pains with my father. Turns out, the academic pressures and high expectations Dad placed on me were eerily similar to what Bill had experienced with his father, and he actually may have had it worse. Before he left for Portsmouth Abbey, their relationship had deteriorated, relegated to incessant arguments and miscommunications. At times they didn't even speak to each other. So as a young, precocious high school student, Bill decided to be proactive and work on a resolution.

He wrote his father a long letter, highlighting some of the issues he felt were pushing them apart. The letter described the intense academic pressure he felt as a kid and how that had a negative impact on him. Perhaps most importantly, Bill told his Dad how much he loved him and wanted to open up the lines of communication so that they could have a healthier relationship than what they currently had. Not long after Bill sent the letter, during a visit home, his father told him in person that he had received it, read it, and was looking forward to talking to him more about it someday. The boating accident occurred five days later, and they never got the opportunity to have that conversation. Bill told me in confidence that he was glad he wrote to his father. Even though they never got a chance to talk about it in depth, he told him how he was feeling and his Dad had acknowledged it. He often worried about how he would have felt if his father had passed and he hadn't written the letter at all.

Bill reminded me that like the famous cliché, life was short. You don't know what could happen from day to day, and if I expected the issues between my father and me to be resolved, I should take steps to initiate the conversation myself. I took his advice to heart. Not only was he my oldest friend, but also he knew our family very well. So on a quiet spring night, I sat in a local café in Midtown Atlanta and decided that my birthday present to my father that year was going to be a long, heartfelt letter.

My fingers toiled for three hours to construct that letter. I don't think I realized how long I had been waiting to write it, or how many issues I had repressed over the years, because my tears were flowing as freely as the words scribed on paper. I was in therapy, a church of sorts, where I could write and have my words heard by a static legal pad that would not speak back or pass judgment upon me. The handwritten memo birthed that night was about six legal pad pages long, front and back. In it I spoke honestly about my disappointment that he wasn't around to support me in my extracurricular activities during grade school and high school. I disclosed my resentment towards him for never being pleased with or recognizing anything I accomplished. I even boldly declared that he should be proud of me at this point in life. Here I was going to medical school and following in his footsteps by being a physician. My attraction to men could never be a bad thing or detract from that reality. His youngest son could be strung out on drugs, a high school dropout, or just an unmotivated lazy twenty-something who was staying at home with him and my mom. I wasn't perfect, but by most standards I had turned out pretty damn good. I ended the letter expressing my hope that he could move past his disapproval of my sexuality and just accept me for who I was. No matter how he felt about me, I would always love him as my father.

I sent the letter out a week before Dad's birthday, and called him on his day to wish him well. He didn't mention it when we spoke, and I didn't ask him if he had received it or what he thought about it. I figured he could initiate that conversation if he was so inclined. Consistent with his spirit, he never discussed it with me, but my mother did. She told me he spent time alone reading it, and that he was moved to tears. To this day we have yet to talk about the content of that letter, but after his birthday in 1995, things changed. His physical health improved, and Mom ceased calling me with weekly-worried reports about abnormal lab tests and lingering colds. Our flow as two human beings, father and son, also took a turn for the better. Conversations on the phone became longer, and the hugs and morning/evening kisses that were a daily ritual growing up suddenly reemerged. He was welcoming his son back, and I happily returned home with open arms, thankful to reconnect with the man who always inspired me. My warmest gratitude, however, was reserved for my good friend Bill Brazell – the one person who woke me up and encouraged me to stop and say "hi" instead of letting my own father continue to pass me by.

11

Don't get old

In the summer of 2000, New York City's congested blocks of concrete were humid and uncomfortable. Bodies sweated side-by-side on dingy subway platforms in anticipation of the rush of cool air when the A train's doors opened to bring them downtown. Pregnant stroller commandos ran people over and sideswiped legs trying to get their children on the next subterranean vessel. Unsolicited stimuli from faux blind passengers handing out cards pleading for money interrupted my daily read. Marginally-talented singers, dancers, and other artists ensured that every train commute would never be without intrusion. People were claustrophobically clustered by necessity and jockeyed for space while I desperately tried my best to ignore them. Everything about Manhattan was getting on my last good nerve. And I wouldn't have had it any other way.

Standing on His Shoulders

I was completing the first year of a Preventive Medicine Residency at the New York City Department of Health at the turn of the century. West Harlem was where I laid my head, on the third floor of a brownstone at 142nd and Convent Avenue. The building was owned by a maternal school teacher, Sandra Davoll, who lived there with her gifted daughter Anika. They became my family away from home in that historic Sugar Hill neighborhood, the one that pre-dated the Bill Clinton-inspired corporate infestation with gentrified residents. Yellow taxi cab drivers were still scared to take fares north of 125th street, and you had to trick them into taking you there. Green cabs didn't even exist. Brownstone tenants respected themselves, the community, and each other. You could still walk down the streets, close your eyes and breathe in the spirits of Langston, Countee, and Zora circulating in the air.

I had just completed my Internal Medicine residency, turned thirty, and was beginning to embrace a newfound maturity. My mind was fixated on completing a master's in public health and a successful medical career was on the cusp of realization. The tortuous years of delayed gratification that define the lives of so many physicians-in-training were coming to a close for me. I even took a trip to Puerto Rico for Memorial Day Weekend with a few friends. We had such a good time I promised myself from that day forward I would never let another year go by without at least once enjoying the warm sands and peaceful rhythmic waves of a Caribbean beach. I came home from that vacation on top of the world.

That all changed the morning of Friday, June 2, 2000. I didn't have class or clinic that morning, so I had decided to sleep in and get some rest after a few hectic days back at work. My answering machine, an archaic Panasonic contraption placed mere feet away from my bed, was turned off, silent and nonthreatening. Somewhere between seven and eight in the morning the phone announced itself, abruptly interrupting my peaceful slumber. I simply ignored the first round of rings, pretending that the annoying sound was nothing but a bad dream. But it kept ringing and ringing. My next thought was that whoever was calling that early in the morning had some nerve trying to reach me at that hour. So I was going to announce my displeasure by not answering. That'll show them. But after three separate calls that rang about twenty times each, I woke up, turned off the ringer, and put my answering machine back on so this anonymous caller could at least leave a message. Now that I was awake, I thought I might as well start my day and took a shower.

When I returned from the bathroom, my answering machine light was blinking. I pressed play, and the distressed, rarely heard voice of my sister emerged from the speaker.

"David, this is Michelle. Dad's had a stroke and Mom has been trying to call you all morning but said she couldn't get through, so she wanted me to try. When you get this message give her a call."

I felt a cold chill run through my entire body. *This* was the phone call I had been ignoring all morning, my mother trying to let me know that Dad just had a stroke. My mind recalled the multiple life events where the chinks in his physical armor were revealed: The mysterious illness with his low blood count and liver abnormalities when I returned home for Christmas break; the herniated discs in his back that required surgery just two years earlier; the long history of hypertension that was supposedly well controlled; and the accumulation of thousands of long days of surgeries and midnight calls to the hospital pulling him away from his family and prioritizing his own personal health. It seemed that the demanding life of a top surgeon was finally exacting its physical toll on my father's body.

I immediately called my mother who, in a shaky voice, told me that Dad had actually been feeling under the weather the night before, but they both thought it was his blood pressure. He checked it at a local fire station, and it was normal, so he just went to bed. In the middle of the night, however, he woke up feeling generally unsettled but couldn't pinpoint what it was. Mom saw his face and told him then that it looked like he had a mild facial droop on one side. He replied, "Donna, it is likely just a mini-stroke," in his typically dismissive, Haitian-surgeon-all-knowing manner. He then took a hot shower and went back to bed. At 6 a.m., he woke up as he normally had for years, ready for a full day of surgery and clinic. When he tried to rise out of bed, his legs buckled under him like straw stilts and he collapsed to the floor, unable to pull himself up. Mom called 911 and they brought him to St. Clare's Hospital, where he had served as Chief of Surgery for close to twenty years. He was diagnosed with an acute stroke and transferred to Ellis Hospital for additional tests and treatment.

Mom sounded horrible. She didn't seem to know how serious it was or whether he would live or die, only that he was in the intensive care unit and they were monitoring him closely. I hung up the phone and prepared to drive home as soon as possible. A strange tingling violently knotted my stomach. I had dreaded this day when Dad's clichéd phrase that he "wouldn't always be around" came true. I called my cousin Danielle, who worked as a traveling nurse at the New York Hospital where I did my residency. When I told her what happened, she selflessly dropped what she was doing and drove up with me to Schenectady. Our journey that day felt longer than the usual two and a half hour pilgrimage to upstate New York from New York City. We couldn't take in the scenic foliage on the Garden State Parkway and New York Thruway with the same frivolous enjoyment that accompanied my trips with Dad during college. The leaves on trees looked cold and lifeless, and I couldn't stop thinking dreadful thoughts about what could be happening to my father.

Ellis Hospital was again the setting. The place where my mother and father met and now where his mortality would be tested. My heart was racing as Danielle and I rushed through the stale corridors to the nurses' station where my mother was waiting. She looked defeated as she made her way towards me, her emerald eyes now tinted ruby red, fatigued, and sunken in. Her typically proud shoulders slumped in reluctant resignation during this sudden turn of events. We embraced tightly, both of us tearing up, as she brought me to Dad's room. I cautiously walked in, greeted by the eerie cadence of vital signs monitors and IV medications fluttering in my ear. The room was pasty white, from the floor to the ceiling. Only the rich brown of my father's skin over his sheets interrupted the bleached monotony.

Dad actually looked peaceful lying in that neurological intensive care unit bed, not unlike how I remembered him during summer vacations as a child when he was curled up reading a book. Here was the man who spent his entire life working tirelessly in small, upstate New York hospitals. He was incessantly stressed, on call, and at the whim of unpredictable surgical emergencies that could interrupt his life at any time of the day. Seeing him motionless in that bed made me thankful that for now he was actually resting. He probably would have never stopped working unless he physically couldn't, and that was the exact reality he was now facing. I approached him, slowly reaching out to hold the wrinkled hand that could narrate countless stories of lives it helped save. His eyes opened, gazing upon me as he smiled in surprise and appreciation. I kissed him softly on the cheek.

"How are you Dad?" I said, fighting back tears.

"Oh, I'm OK son." He sighed. "Your father's getting old."

He closed his eyes again.

The neurologists taking care of Dad told me he suffered a type of stroke called Wallenberg Syndrome. He was born with a narrow blood vessel in the back of his brain, and over time a clot had formed, stopping the flow of oxygen. This type of stroke was not the kind where someone gets weak on one side of their body and has slurred speech. The stroke Dad had affected his cerebellum, the area of the brain that controls balance, coordination, vision, and swallowing functions. If his stroke had been just millimeters lower, he could have easily died. As it stood, he would require months of extensive physical rehabilitation. Even worse, his days of performing meticulous surgeries were likely numbered. The doctors put him on a blood thinner, gave him aspirin daily, and monitored him closely in the neurological intensive care unit. I knew it was just going to be a waiting game to see how quickly he would recover. As a medical resident, I had cared for many stroke patients, but it was quite a different perspective watching Dad go through the same ordeal. I felt helpless to do anything about it.

In trying times, you can always tell how much a man is loved by the individuals who rally around him. This was no truer than when I saw the people who came out of the woodwork to see my father in the hospital. Family, friends, patients, co-workers, and everyone who knew him or had interacted with him wanted to show support in his time of need. Over the next few days, Dad's condition steadily improved, and his gregarious personality returned with a vengeance. It was nothing short of miraculous watching him hold court from his bed in the hospital room when guests would arrive, like a king on his throne. He would sit upright, narrating fantastical stories and colorful jokes to his visitors. If I had shut my eyes, I would've thought he was at home or interacting with colleagues in the operating room. Some of his patients would even come to check up on him, only to start talking about their own medical problems. And oddly enough, Dad would actually sit and listen to them, as if his hospital room was his clinic, and they were returning for a follow-up visit with him after surgery. Even as a patient, Dad was still a healer extraordinaire and his visitors were more than willing to satisfy this part of his spirit.

I was initially angry at how these seemingly self-centered people came to ostensibly check up on him, only to dump their own personal problems in his lap, despite his obvious weakened condition. Then I watched how happy it made Dad to engage them in this manner. He cherished the role he played in their lives, even when he was a recovering stroke patient in the intensive care unit. This probably kept his mind off his own health struggles and helped him maintain a semblance of normalcy during a chaotic situation over which he had little control. So I let go of my resentment towards these human parasites after a couple of days. Who was I to deny Dad from coping with his illness the best way he knew how?

Eventually we had to ask the hospital staff to restrict visitors to immediate family so that Dad could rest. He got weak quickly, even from just talking, and people either didn't recognize it or chose to ignore it. He wouldn't ask them to leave for fear of being perceived as rude and not appreciative of them coming – reluctance he chalked up to his "Haitian ways." So my mother and I had to be the bad guys, roles neither of us minded assuming. I only have one father, who dedicated himself to the community's medical needs and concerns for years. I would be damned if I would let them place their needs above his own when *he* was the patient this time. This was one of the first times I fully recognized how my father's altruistic nature could be addictive and self-destructive all at the same time. How the personal calling and desire to heal others could easily be prioritized over healing oneself. While

Dad may have personally felt unable to put up boundaries between him and the people who adored him, I was more than happy to help him draw those lines of distinction.

After several days, the doctors decided that Dad's condition had improved enough that they stopped his blood thinners and transferred him to the hospital's rehab facility. I thought it strange that they would send him straight from the neurological intensive care unit to rehab without transitioning him to a regular hospital floor for monitoring for a day or two. Instead of voicing my concern, I remained silent, as he looked so much better and I didn't want to diffuse his exuberance over the prospect of leaving the hospital. I also didn't want to come off as the jerk family member with medical training who always second guesses every decision the staff makes in an effort to control the situation. Being on the other end of that equation can be quite an irritating experience. I decided to give the medical team a break and not let my subjective bias toward Dad cloud their clinical judgment or my own.

Dad's transfer to the rehab facility seemed to be the perfect time for me to return to New York City and get my affairs in order. I had already graduated and received my public health degree, but had yet to complete the Preventive Medicine Residency curricula. My residency director gave me two months off so I could help my parents with Dad's recovery. I packed my belongings for an extended home visit like I was preparing for a funeral as my previously care-free New York life metamorphosed before my eyes. The excitement of walking amongst vibrant New Yorkers was gone, replaced by an infection with a morose spiritual virus I couldn't shake. I had suddenly morphed into one of the countless urban zombies mulling around to and fro. None of the things I felt were important seemed so anymore. I just longed to get home and be with my parents as soon as possible.

Unfortunately, my lower back had other plans. While walking down Astor Place in the lower East side, it decided to subject me to the most excruciating pain I had ever felt. It came on suddenly and sharp, lacerating my skin and piercing my nerves until I contorted into a mass of flesh, bone, and muscle in the middle of the sidewalk. Strangers passed by and stared at me without offering assistance. I managed to slowly pull myself up and hobbled to the A train and got back up to my third floor walkup in Harlem. I began taking Motrin like they were delicious gummy bears, now fully appreciative of how stress could impact the physical health of a Malebranche man. I had been running nonstop, trying to be the strong one for my family during Dad's time of need, and hadn't taken any time to breathe and take care of myself. My back pain flaring up at this precise moment was not a coincidence. It was simply my body's way of letting me know I needed to sit my ass down. Reluctantly, I listened. I realized that as much as I have emulated my father in many ways, his proclivity for ignoring his own health issues was not one of them.

I delayed my return to upstate New York for a couple of days. During my recuperation, however, Mom called. As soon as I heard her voice, I knew the news was bad. Dad had suffered another stroke less than 24 hours after his transfer to the rehabilitation center. At 3 a.m., he notified the nurse that he was experiencing blurry vision and dizziness worse than when he first had the stroke. The nurse told him she would call the physician assistant but that they couldn't get the doctor at the moment. My father, the former Chief of Surgery, and one of the fiercest competitors the world has ever seen, was not going to settle for that. From his rehabilitation room, he called one of his good friends who is a cardiologist at four o'clock in the morning and implored him to come by and check him out. His friend arrived at the rehab center, saw my father's symptoms for himself, and ordered another MRI of his brain. Dad had suffered an extension of the previous stroke and was immediately transferred back to the neurological intensive care unit.

So several heating pads, Motrin tablets, and a few muscle relaxants later, I was packed and driving back to upstate New York. This time I resolved to stay as long as it took to help Dad get back on his feet, both literally and figuratively. I returned to Schenectady not really knowing how or if he was going to fully recover, and with uncertainty about what life would be like for him and the rest of our family. When I arrived at the hospital, I was surprised to see a strange man who only vaguely resembled my father lying in his bed. His face was gaunt and weathered, no longer the carefree entertainer of any and all visitors to his bedside I had left just a few days prior. He wasn't the Messiah of the Operating Room anymore. He was a fragile, aging man suffering profusely from the complications of a stroke. It tore me up to see him that uncomfortable, and I knew this time he would not make it out of the woods so easily. The doctors put him back on the blood thinners that they probably should have never taken him off of in the first place. My anger towards them for making that decision was overshadowed by my concern for Dad's recovery. I spent my first days back commuting between the hospital and Albany Medical School's library, ingesting all articles on strokes so I could ensure he was getting the proper treatment. I became more vocal in demanding he get the proper care he deserved, not concerned anymore about how the medical staff felt about me. This was my Dad, and it was obvious that being a former surgeon at the hospital where he was currently being treated didn't seem to influence the quality of care he was receiving. He needed someone to be his voice right now. That voice had to come from me.

I spent a lot of time with Dad during his second hospital admission, desperately trying to distract his attention from the stark reality of his illness. Call it our forced version of the quality time we had missed while I was growing up if you will. The important thing was that it was time together. He spoke passionately about returning to surgery while in re-hab, a notion I couldn't envision given his current state of affairs. A 68-year-old man who couldn't even walk and had lost sensation in his left arm would be a longshot to successfully navigate dissecting a human body. I tried my best to keep our conversations light and optimistic, for if ever there was a time he needed a "glass half full" perspective, it was now. Dad saw that my back was bothering me from his bedside, and being the consummate caretaker, referred me to a close friend of his who was a local physical therapist. On my first visit, she told me I was having muscle spasms that were pushing my lower spine to the left and prescribed several weeks of focused back exercises, heating pads, and Motrin. As I helped Dad recover from his stroke, I began my own healing process as well.

Several days later, Dad's condition improved and he was discharged back to the rehab center to the exact same bed where the previous mishap had taken place. My mother and I were a little suspicious of the facility's competence at this point, but also realized that inpatient rehab was a necessary evil in the recovery process. We would just have to be fully prepared to scream, yell, and beat somebody's ass if they weren't taking care of him properly. He was scheduled to stay there for several weeks until the therapists felt he was able to continue his rehab at home. This didn't make him happy at all, but I didn't mind spending the additional time with him. It had been so long since I had been home with my parents that I basked in the glow of spending the days at rehab with my father, and the nights at home with my mother. I was blessed with the opportunity to experience them all over again, but this time as a man. They seemed comforted that one of their children could be there during Dad's crisis. Michelle was in her third trimester of pregnancy with her first child at the time. She was not medically cleared to fly on a plane to come home from California, so I tried my best to hold down the fort for both of us.

The only hiccup in my father's recovery while in rehab was when he aspirated some of his saliva and developed pneumonia. I remember the night he was in the worst condition we had seen him in during the whole ordeal. The physicians caring for him had just put him on antibiotics and we could do nothing but wait and see. He laid prone and immobile, coughing uncontrollably and trying desperately to catch his breath when he could. Mom decided to stay overnight at the rehab center to be by his side. As I prepared to go home, she grabbed my arm.

"Do you think he could die overnight?" she asked.

As I watched the sweat slowly trickle down my father's head in his feverish state, I desperately wanted to reassure her that everything was going to be ok. I knew that wasn't possible.

"Mom, I don't know. If he doesn't improve overnight, they may have to get him back to a hospital bed," I told her.

I went home thinking of my father lying in that cold impersonal room and if that was the last time I would see him. Mom remained by his side. She stayed with him that night fearful that it might be their last together. Whether trekking to Mexico to help him return to the United States or spotting him as he carried Michelle and me up the stairs to our beds – she had always been there with him. It was the two of them against the world.

Dad responded to the antibiotics and never had to be transferred back to the hospital. His personality and spirit came back as he continued to improve. Over the next couple of weeks in rehab, I got to meet several of his closest friends and colleagues who would come by for hours at a time and reminisce fondly, swapping war stories about Ellis hospital and St. Clare's glory days. During quiet times, I would sit alone with him and watch baseball, basketball, and golf on TV. Tiger Woods was slaughtering the competition at the

U.S. Open that year. We sat together and marveled with pride as a young Black golfer, who shared a close relationship with his own father, won one of golf's most prestigious tournaments. As we watched Tiger tearfully hug his father after his well-earned victory, I recalled my medical school graduation ceremony just five years earlier. After I crossed that stage, held that diploma in my hand, and proudly recited the Hippocratic Oath, the one person I really wanted to get a hug from was Dad. He was my primary inspiration in achieving that goal and taking the life path I did. I imagined that Tiger felt the same way as he wrapped his arms around the man who inspired him to be the best golfer in the world.

Being away from New York City was not a bad thing for me at the time. I was burnt out from almost five straight years of residency, so it was good to slow things down and be reminded about how important family was. I did miss my close friends, who are like an extended family to me. When they suggested driving up to visit one weekend, we arranged it to be the same weekend Dad would be granted his first time away from the hospital and rehab since the stroke. They were giving him a day pass, so we brought him up to the lake house in Galway. Dad was restricted to a wheelchair but sat with my mother and three of my closest friends, Doug, Steve, and Marlon. We joined together to laugh, eat, and talk for hours. It was the first time in weeks I had seen Dad genuinely happy. He was human again. It was a day the two of us would never forget.

My father has always perked up when I bring friends to visit. He usually has a lecture prepared for us about being

Standing on His Shoulders

Black men in America and how important it is for all of us to succeed and achieve our goals and dreams. This time was no different, as he seemed to have an even broader perspective on life since the stroke. My friends sat as they usually do, charmed and intrigued by his advice and stories of life experiences. For me it was a particular blessing to hear these stories and lectures again given everything that he had been through in the past several weeks. When I was younger I used to roll my eyes and sigh when he would try to teach me something. I now watched intently as his animated face glanced back and forth at all of ours, and the inflection of his voice rose and fell with renewed purpose. I listened with the intent that only life experience can bring, seeing with much fuller appreciation what a truly amazing man my Dad was, and how quickly he could've been taken away.

When Dad finally left rehab and came home for good, it was like we had won the lottery. He was still in the wheelchair, but clearly on the path to full recovery. I spent the remainder of my two months there, helping Mom with his everyday care and assisting him with his rehab goals. As he gained strength and went from a wheelchair to a walker, we spent a lot of time together outside, kicking a soccer ball around to improve his balance and coordination. Mom would anxiously watch the two of us, standing several feet apart, as we laughed and kicked the ball back and forth. Always the cautious and nervous person, she would plead with him to be careful and not overdo it with his rehab activities. You couldn't stop my father at that time, or even tell him to slow down. He could see the light at the end of the tunnel, and visions of his first grandchild, Skylar Rose, were driving him to push himself. I would encourage Dad to go further than what the physical therapist expected, remembering how his high expectations of me sustained me and kept me focused in life for so many years. He would gingerly stroll into the kitchen where Mom and I were sitting, holding onto the counter and practice walking back and forth alternating hands until he could balance himself on his own. A man possessed with a rejuvenated spirit, he appeared truly joyful in witnessing his own progress in the face of adversity.

To this day, it's truly amazing to see how far Dad has come in terms of his physical recovery from a stroke that would have left many wanting to give up on life. He calls June 2, 2000 his "second birthday" and commemorates the occasion every year. I was just honored to be there to witness his rebirth at 68 years young, and help him with any physical or emotional support I could. The same way he and my mother have always been present for me.

12

WITH HIS HANDS

When I was a child, Dad would fondly reminisce about his native Haiti and Anse-à-Veau, the small rustic town adorned by pristine beaches and azure water that raised him until his early twenties. He always spoke of the island's majestic beauty on many levels: as the first independent Black republic in the world; its abundant resources and fertile land; and the resilience of Haitian people despite decades of repeated social, economic, and political hardships. These remembrances, always told in his rich accent and with a vibrant *joie de vivre*, starkly contrasted with the uniformly depressing media narratives of Haiti as merely an island of poverty, HIV, political corruption, and natural disasters.

As a family, we often discussed taking a trip to my father's birthplace, but it never seemed to be the right time – outbreaks of violence, infectious diseases, or political instability always made traveling to Haiti an unappealing option for a family vacation. As years passed by, the fickle and ephemeral circumstances of life made this simple task of taking a trip to Haiti a near impossible challenge. My schooling and career path took me through New Jersey, Chicago, Michigan, and New York City before finally landing in Atlanta to pursue an academic medical career. My sister traveled through California and Hawaii, and back again to California to practice law and raise her own family. Through all this, my parents remained in upstate New York, the place they have called home for close to fifty years. We never went to Haiti as we had planned, and I never learned the Kreyol dialect. I was a first generation Haitian-American without much of a connection to Haiti. I feared that a trip to the home of part of my ancestral heritage would never happen.

That all changed in 2011 when I was presented with the opportunity to be part of an academic medical team that goes to Haiti twice a year to do relief work. It was the chance of a lifetime to use my medical expertise in addressing the lingering medical and public health consequences of the devastating earthquake of 2010, while also walking on the soil that nurtured my father. He had instilled a tenacious work ethic and sense of resiliency in me during adversity at an early age. These sensibilities course through my veins, comprise the air I breathe, and constitute the intricate fabric of my being. They exist in me because of him. They exist in me because Haiti exists. The decision to return to my father's homeland at the ripe age of forty-two was an easy one to make.

Standing on His Shoulders

Working at our mobile clinic sites each day in the rural Central Plateau area of Haiti was a professional and personal challenge for me. The lingering devastation of the earthquake hung in the air like thick caustic fumes. An emerging cholera epidemic inundated the local hospitals with droves of sick people relegated to makeshift tents disguised as hospital beds. As I navigated this landscape, I tried my best to address every patient's concern and teach the eager young medical students. All the while I was fumbling through my broken Kreyol and relying heavily on the translators to compensate for my linguistic limitations. Even with my medical and public health experience, I felt woefully inadequate and ill prepared for what Haiti needed. This slightly paranoid and insecure first generation Haitian-American was putting a flimsy bandage of Tylenol, antibiotics, and oral rehydration solution on the hemorrhaging gunshot wound of Haiti's devastating medical, social, and structural ills. I could see the disappointment in the custom officer's face when he read my last name and subsequently learned I didn't speak Kreyol. I could hear the disdain in our van drivers' voices as they sucked their teeth at me when they realized the same thing. Yes, my clinical acumen was intact, but I couldn't shake the feeling that I was somehow dishonoring my family name by being the Americanized Malebranche who was blatantly displaying his cultural incompetence in his father's birthplace. My colleagues and the translators joked that my English-Kreyol handbook never left my side the entire week of our mission. They didn't get it. For me, this was much more than a professional trip.

After our third day in clinic, during a quiet evening of games and good conversation at our compound, one of the community health workers brought in a Haitian teenager who had a foreign object stuck in his ear. He was a towering young man, well over six feet tall and lanky. I quietly sat on the periphery as everyone surrounded this new and unexpected patient. We discovered that half of a Q-tip had broken off in his ear and was causing him a great deal of pain. One of the nearby hospitals had seen him earlier, only to send him home because the electricity went out and they didn't have sufficient light to aid them in properly extracting it. The health worker didn't know where else to go, so he brought him to the American contingent of doctors and medical students to see if there was anything we could do.

We set up a makeshift examining space on a dining table, and our pediatrician began irrigating his ear in an attempt to expand the cotton tip and make it easier to remove. Several medical students grabbed some lighting equipment and a hemostat from our van. My previous irrational embarrassment and feelings of inadequacy had me paralyzed, so I simply sat back, secretly hoping that they wouldn't call me over. Our medical team and several local townspeople hovered over the young man like hospital staff smothering patients during a cardiac arrest. I consciously chose to be an impartial observer on the other side of the room, commenting to a medical student sitting next to me,

"I'm not getting involved in this."

No sooner had those words escaped my lips when someone bellowed from the crowd, almost as if on cue.

Standing on His Shoulders

"David, we need you over here!"

I walked over and looked in the teen's right ear, the cotton swab wedged tightly between the fleshy walls of his ear canal. The area around the swab was inflamed, bleeding, and the jagged edge of the wooden stick was threatening to puncture his eardrum. Remembering my manners, I stopped looking and introduced myself to him, shaking his hand.

"Mwen rele David Malebranche. Kijan ou rele?" I asked.

"M rele Patrice" he replied, doing an admirable job of masking the discomfort of having a foreign body lodged in his ear and the growing spectacle swirling around him. Was that me speaking very basic Kreyol without a stutter? Our pediatrician's concerned glance snapped me back into focus.

"You got any other ideas on how to get this out?" she asked.

I had none, so she said she would let me know if she needed any help. I returned to the other side of the room and watched as she continued working on Patrice's ear. The whole scene reminded me of how American media covers the story a small child's untimely fall down a well, complete with a concerned crowd waiting in anticipatory silence as the rescue workers concentrate on their efforts. It wasn't long before I was called back over.

"David, we need you again."

Our pediatrician looked at me in an exasperated fashion, wiping the sweat trickling down her forehead from the oppressively humid Caribbean night air.

"I've tried to get it out a couple of times, but I'm worried about puncturing his eardrum. Wanna give it a shot?" she asked.

Without thinking, my dry mouth had already fixed itself to say "sure" as I made my way over to Patrice, hemostat in hand. I gazed at the sea of young, curious, and inexperienced faces of future doctors-to-be surrounding me. I was the senior physician to whom they were looking for guidance and leadership. What if I failed Patrice? What if I damaged his eardrum trying to help him? What kind of example would I be giving these students if I were unable to retrieve the swab? I felt like I had been catapulted back in time to my first day of internship when a hospital nurse called me at 3 a.m. to evaluate a patient with shortness of breath. As I approached the middle aged woman, hunched over on her hospital bed, laboring to breathe and using all of her accessory muscles, I kept thinking "someone get a doctor." Then I realized that I *was* the doctor.

One of the medical students helped fix my headlight as I looked down at Patrice's strained youthful face and desperately tried to swallow my wounded pride from the past few days and focus on the task at hand. I took a slow, deep breath and instead of thinking about myself, the social problems in Haiti, or out-of-place Q-tips, I thought about my father. I thought about his buoyant stories of riding horseback as a young physician to local Haitian villages with medical bag in hand, providing care to those suffering from tuberculosis, cholera, and other infectious diseases. I thought about his journey to the United States and surgical training in New York City. I envisioned the fellowship he did in upstate New York and subsequent private surgical practice he set up there despite English not being his first language. I imagined him and my mother tirelessly and unselfishly raising my sister and me the best they could so we could stand on their shoulders and see the world. I pictured the thousands of times he took a hemostat, scalpel, or other surgical instrument in his capable hands to help someone in far more dire circumstances than what Patrice was experiencing at that moment. I felt those same hands guiding mine as I delicately reached in Patrice's ear with the hemostat. On the second attempt, I slowly extracted a bloody, wax-covered broken off wooden swab. The room erupted with ebullient cheers as Patrice looked up at me, flashing the brightest smile of surprise, relief, and excitement that only an eighteen-year-old can. He quickly stood up, shook my hand firmly and we embraced.

I found out later that Patrice was actually the son of the community health worker who brought him to our compound that night. He was the brightest student in his class and had plans to go to Cuba to study medicine after he finished school. I watched intently as his family enveloped him with love, pride, and belief in his unlimited potential – the same way I imagined Tante Jeanne and Grand Dede embraced, nurtured, and believed in the future of a young man from Anse-à-Veau over six decades earlier. Patrice left our compound that evening to return to his teenage life, unaware that one of his elders, a retired Haitian surgeon in upstate New York, had just laid hands on him.

On our last night in the Central Plateau, one of our Haitian female translators, Marie, pulled me away from the group after dinner.

"David, I know you were not born here like your father, and we don't always hear good things about Black men in

America here in Haiti. But I must say that it has been a joy to work with you and witness you serve as one of the head physicians on this trip. And the way you have picked up Kreyol in the past week has been amazing."

She paused, her eyes becoming cloudy as she looked through me.

"You have inspired me. I'm proud to call you my Haitian brother."

Tears streamed down my face as she hugged me, and I felt my father's embrace from 1600 miles away.

13

Becoming a Father

His email arrived in my inbox folder with little fanfare, like the faintest tugging on my lab coat. The generic title, "Medical Advice," blended in and nestled so comfortably between the numerous other emails that it might otherwise have slipped unnoticed into my spam folder. But the text of this message was different, the words deliberate and dire, desperately begging for me to stop what I was doing and pay attention to him.

"I know you don't know me," the first line read, "but my name is James. I'm twenty-five years old, live in Florida, and I have AIDS. My doctors here are giving me medications that are making me sick and I don't think they know what they are doing. *Please, I need your help.*"

After a decade of working as an attending physician at Grady Hospital in Atlanta, one truism I learned is that offering medical recommendations on the Internet is a tricky business - especially to someone whom you've never seen as a patient. It's something like "Monday morning quarterbacking," when we all suddenly become professional athletes and say what *we* would have done to win the game for our favorite football team last Sunday. During the email exchanges that followed, I was careful not to give James specific medical advice, always ending with "Go talk to your doctor." I genuinely felt I wasn't helping him at all, so when he showed up as a new patient in my Atlanta practice a couple of months later, to say I was surprised would be a gross understatement.

James was an unassuming young Black man: 5 feet, 6 inches tall, 140 pounds, with light brown skin, full curly hair, and deep set eyes that mirrored an old soul kind of sadness incongruous with his youth. When I called his name, he wearily stood up, but managed to flash a broad and hopeful smile as he reached out to shake my hand.

"I'm James, the one who sent you the email from Florida."

I quickly made the connection. "You came all this way?" I said.

"I used to come to this clinic years ago when I lived here. My friends recommended you, so after I Googled you and saw you were legit, I decided to move back," he explained. His voice was confident and determined, with a tone and cadence strikingly similar to my own. I liked him immediately.

James wasn't close to any of his family in Atlanta, and primarily relied on friends for social support. His biological father had been an alcoholic who died of cirrhosis complications years ago. "We were never close," he stated matter-of-factly, a phrase uttered far too frequently by my Black male patients when discussing their biological fathers. During his first clinical visit with me, James' only complaint was diarrhea. Despite his T cell count of less than thirty, he didn't fit the clinical picture of someone suffering from AIDS-related diarrhea. His cheeks were full, his weight was appropriate for his height, and all his preliminary labs were normal. I chose to treat his diarrhea conservatively with diet and other behavioral recommendations, and we agreed to meet again in one month after his labs came back to determine the best HIV treatment options for him. Only two days passed before James called my office again.

"The diarrhea is getting worse. I've been to two emergency rooms, but they both sent me home." He lamented.

I told him to immediately go to Grady Hospital's emergency room. He followed my instructions and was admitted. A day later, James' diarrhea mysteriously stopped, his labs were again all normal, and he was expediently discharged home. The whole story was a little baffling to me. Here was a young man with AIDS complaining of daily diarrhea but physically, clinically, and lab-wise he looked fine. Was this a case of the "boy who cried wolf"? Was he just trying to make a case for disability, a common practice at our clinic? On my way to admit another patient to my own hospital service, I ran into James in the hospital atrium. His glowing demeanor was replaced by uncombed hair and disheveled clothes.

"The doctors called security on me because I wouldn't go home," he said dejectedly, fighting back tears. "But I'm just gonna go to another emergency room. I *know* something's wrong, even if no one believes me," he pleaded.

As if on cue, my pager interrupted us – it was my resident contacting me about our next hospital admission. I had to go.

"James, call me on Monday if you don't feel better. We'll figure out what to do," I said while hurriedly making my way to the elevator. His eyes didn't leave me as the doors closed. I felt helpless, and a small part of me was even beginning to regret answering his email in the first place.

Monday morning greeted me with several new phone messages, all from James. Two more days. Two more emergency rooms. Two more discharges. Amidst a barrage of coughs and groans, his raspy voice muttered on the last voicemail, "My friends say I'm just trying to get attention. Call me, doc. I don't know what to do."

"*I don't know what to do.*"

I recalled saying those exact words over the phone to my father in 1991, after traveling eighteen hours on a crowded, pungent Amtrak train from Chicago to New York for a medical school interview. I had just been questioned by a rude, hurried surgeon who was thirty minutes late and only met with me for five minutes before excusing himself for his next operation. Disappointed, I asked the admissions office receptionist for another interview, and was abruptly told I would have to come back next month. I almost followed her instructions, but repeating an eighteen-hour train ride there and back again was not an option. I didn't have the money or the time to take off from my restaurant job at the time. So I called my father because *I didn't know what to do*. His stern voice issued a distinct order: "Son, you march right back into that admissions office and do not leave until you receive the interview you deserve."

I returned and pled my case with the receptionist until the Director of Admissions, whose office was directly behind the receptionist, overheard our conversation and offered to interview me himself right there on the spot. Turned out he was also a Princeton alumnus, and we ended up engaged in a forty-five-minute discourse about politics, the climate of racial and gender diversity at Princeton, and the future of medicine. I boarded the train back to Chicago feeling good about getting the interview I deserved, and for actually learning something from my Harvard college interview fiasco. Several months later, I received a letter of acceptance from that very school.

For one week, James had been imploring me to hear him, and I hadn't made the time to do so. I called my father once, and he knew exactly what to say. I decided to admit James to my hospital team for a colonoscopy and repeat the stool cultures until we figured out what was going on. Within a day we discovered the cause of his diarrhea, a parasite called *Cryptosporidium.* This parasite, while common, can be deadly for people living with AIDS. James' symptoms had a cause and everyone had missed it, including me. I humbly entered James' hospital room to tell him the news and apologize for what I perceived as my own failings as his physician. To my surprise, his radiant smile reemerged as soon as he saw me, eclipsing the orange sunlight from the hospital window as he squeezed my hand tightly.

"Thank you for believing me," he beamed.

James got better as we treated the parasite and put him on HIV medications. A few days later, we sent him home. This time he left with a definitive diagnosis, treatment plan, and most importantly, a chance to be twenty-five again.

When I was a boy, I remember my father taking me to St. Clare's Hospital where he worked as a chief surgeon. We traveled through endless pristine hallways, past the smell of the testosterone-laden surgeons' lounge, and amidst a constant parade of faceless workers in green scrubs. I felt safe and protected as he held my hand and guided me through those hospital corridors - the same way he guided me through my transition into manhood. I used to wonder if his patients looked at him the same way. How did he navigate being such a loving father to me and a mentor to the myriad patients who were looking to him for much more than surgical precision and medication prescriptions? There's no right answer to that question, but as I get older, I can more fully appreciate how challenging it is being dedicated to your role as a savior to your patients and coexist as a devoted parent at the same time. Contrary to what I believed as teenager, Dad did a damn good job.

James came in for a follow-up visit a couple of weeks after being discharged from the hospital. He sported a crisply starched, checkered shirt with French cuffs, dress slacks, and brown wing-tip shoes. A messenger bag hung loosely on his shoulder, completing the projection of youthful swagger that was lost when he was feeling ill. I sat enthralled as he told animated stories of moving back in with his gay uncle, his new boyfriend who is also HIV positive and encourages him to take his medications, and his plans to go back to school and join the gospel choir. He said all of this without the faintest hint of a cough, grimace, or even a groan that would dim the luminous light in his boyish eyes. I was glowing with pride.

Days later I told a good friend of mine about James. I reflected on how numerous other younger Black male patients, students, and doctors-in-training had entered my life over the years seeking treatment, guidance, or mentorship. I remarked, "You know, I think God's preparing me for having my own children."

My friend chuckled.

"David, I think God's trying to tell you these *are* your children."

14

SUNRISE, SUNSET

My father first died on Tuesday, August 13, 2013. His breath became heavy as he sat down on his bed after carrying some antiques up the stairs. That was the last thing Roger Malebranche remembered as he slipped into a black hole of nothingness. His next recollection was his wife of forty-seven years pounding on his chest and screaming his name as his breath suddenly returned. He sat up and began retching as he rejoined this world with equal expediency in which he had just left it. At eighty-one years old, Dad had tried his best in that fleeting moment to check out from this earth with little fanfare or circumstance. But the former nursing student from Granville who turned him down multiple times before agreeing to a first date wasn't ready. Not quite yet.

Standing on His Shoulders

Hours later Dad sat in a cramped hospital room. His bed was adorned with cheap linen over a flimsy mattress that barely provided support for a once strong back, now decimated by herniated discs and rigid surgical adhesions. He was alone with his thoughts of mortality again, made painfully staccato by the constant intrusion of doctors, nurses, and nursing assistants. They ask him to recite his name, scan the wrist band on his arm, dispense his medications, and take his vital signs. They casually inquire about when his last bowel movement was, auscultate his heart and lungs, and provide a sometimes-affected gentle smile or touch to help him feel human again. He fiddles with incessantly screeching hearing aids, desperately trying to hear the muddled explanations of pulmonary emboli, cardiac arrests, and blood thinners that dribble from the mouths of faceless medical drones. The reality of what just happened to this former Messiah of the Operating Room is confusing to him. It strangles his spirit and serves as a somber reminder of the limited time we all have on this earth. All he knows right now is that he had stopped breathing and was ready to transition to an afterlife that seemed to eagerly await him. Now he is back for reasons he doesn't fully comprehend.

I spent a long day visiting with my father in the hospital after he suffered an acute cardiac arrest due to a pulmonary embolism. Unbeknownst to anyone, he had been getting short of breath when walking for several months prior to the arrest, but chalked it up to age and inevitable deconditioning. He never said a word. Not even to Mom. We discussed topics that could take both our collective minds off the dire urgency of the situation facing him: Venus Williams' athletic decline and his newfound appreciation for Serena; the scourge of racism in this country; how medicine is more a business now than an art; and how the fear of discrimination for same-sex couples wanting to demonstrate public displays of affection reminds him of similar fears he had with my mother during the 1960s. His face illuminates when talking about his former surgical practice, and dims dramatically when his mind returns to his current reality. He is a man who, after performing countless surgical procedures and intricate gestures that constitute being a healer on this earth, is now in the position of needing healing himself. He is tired. He is exhausted and beat down in a way I can perhaps never fully understand, and seeing him suffer like this eats at me like an insatiable, gnawing parasite. There's not much I can do to appease the intolerable anguish he feels at this moment except be there with him.

I return to my parents' house in upstate New York, over a decade removed from returning as a thirty-something man when Dad suffered a stroke in 2000. Back then I was just starting my career. Now I am in the throes of it. Circumstances are similar but seem direr this time as I sit outside at the former lake house that has been my parents' permanent home since the stroke. The cool air betrays what should be a humid August night. The lake is calm and serene, and I can barely see any wind filtering through the trees lined up in front of me. I am cognizant of my breathing, the involuntary rhythm of its ebb and flow as it sustains my life. I imagine how much Dad must have struggled to perform this involuntary function we take for granted when he collapsed just days ago. An incessant stream of birds flutter to and fro outside the house, eating from the feeders my mother religiously fills with suet on a weekly basis. They make noises I haven't paid attention to before. The blue jays chirp and squawk as they devour their meal. The hummingbirds make a low pitched rumble before they drink sugar water. The woodpecker flaps its feathers as it burrows its beak in bird feed, frantically searching for the most savory, sugar-coated delicacies.

This mundane picturesque activity all takes place in a business-as-usual fashion as my father lies is in a cold hospital room with the company of his thoughts and a new blood clot taking unwelcome residence in his lungs. He is that "elderly male with a pulmonary embolus" sentence that will carelessly fly from the mouths of the hospital staff, but doesn't quite sum up the nuances of a Haitian man in the winter of his life journey. He is the man who implored me to appreciate the birds' rhythmic humming and fluttering long before I ever could on my own. He is the man who enjoys hearing Luciano Pavarotti and James Brown sing a duet together on YouTube. He is the man who cried in agony over not being there to console his beloved cat Minnie when a stroke kept him away from her for weeks on end. He is the man who still amazes me with his ability to change yet remain remarkably the same. He is the man who would give his own life to make his son happy. He is the man who decided to stay on this earth a little while longer after he felt the resounding thuds of my mother's desperate fists on his chest. He is more than the elderly man with a pulmonary embolus.

After working at Emory University and residing in Atlanta for eleven years, I left the South in October 2012 and returned to familiar northeast surroundings in Philadelphia to take a new position at the University of Pennsylvania. The change afforded me an opportunity to re-evaluate my career while also being geographically closer to my parents. It also allowed me to be more physically present for my parents during times of crises like these. Almost six weeks after my father's blood clot threatened to cut his life short, I returned home for one of my regular monthly visits. Dad's new at-home oxygen machine emits a strange hissing sound at night while it pumps air through his nostrils as he sleeps. The lung issues, not completely resolved, have lingered and made their mark on changing his daily routine. He feels winded when walking short distances, and rarely makes the short pilgrimage up or down stairs anymore. From time to time, despite not complaining of shortness of breath, he will ask Mom to bring the oxygen machine over to his computer during the day. She says nothing when bringing it to him, for she has understood his dialect of verbal denial fluently after all these years.

While still adjusting to these changes during my visits home, I was alerted to a new medical issue plaguing Dad - his stomach was now bothering him. For two weeks he described an aching discomfort in his upper abdomen that he self-diagnosed as an ulcer. He had tried a more bland diet, acid-lowering medications, shrinking portions of meals, and ingesting large gulps of milk when the pain emerged, yet nothing could fully alleviate his discomfort. I returned home to visit on a Friday night and sat down with my parents, my

Dad's brother, Uncle Claude and his wife, Aunt Ruby, who were visiting from Tampa. We discussed Dad's symptoms at the dinner table over dessert. In typical fashion, he downplayed how intense his pain was. He pontificated about how he felt this was a stomach ulcer that was somehow intensifying at night, and he was looking forward to seeing the gastrointestinal doctors to do some testing. They would have to consider what to do about the blood thinners for his clot before performing any procedures on him. It was complicated, but he was resolute in asserting his still-intact knowledge as a physician when assessing his symptoms.

"I am smart enough to diagnose myself," he declared defiantly. No one at the table said a word to dispute his claim. I decided it was time for someone to speak up, that someone being me.

"Dad, no one's going to tell you this, but I will because I love you. You are the smartest man I know, but you seem to always shoot yourself in the foot when it comes to your own health. You did it when you had back pain from the herniated disc. You did it with your stroke. You did it with the blood clot in your lung. Now you're doing it again with this," I stated matter-of-factly.

He looked at me sternly and tried to interrupt me while everyone remained quiet. But I didn't let him.

"Maybe you should have someone evaluate you quickly if it's bothering you that much. If it gets worse, let's just take you to the Emergency Room," I added.

"Why would I want to go to the ER? What are they going to do for me on the weekend?" he questioned.

He had a point.

We left that conversation agreeing that if the pain got worse and wasn't relieved by the milk, we would re-evaluate and consider taking him to the hospital. I know this wasn't a plan he was happy with after spending a miserable week in the hospital just a couple of months earlier, but it was the only feasible option.

Early Sunday morning at 2 a.m., I was awakened by a commotion downstairs. My mother is a loud walker. You can usually hear her footsteps across the floor from any location in the house. Her path becomes especially pronounced when there is urgency in her soul. From my upstairs bedroom, her strides reverberated through the house like the end of days. Something was wrong. I opened my bedroom door and peeked out. My Aunt and Uncle's bedroom door was shut and it was suddenly silent downstairs. A moment passed. Thinking I was dreaming, I returned to bed, only to be startled later by more urgent footsteps accompanied by voices this time. When I opened my bedroom door a second time, a flickering of lights from downstairs peaked through the hallway. I rushed downstairs. My mother was grabbing some milk from the refrigerator.

"Mom, what's going on?" I said.

"He's having the pain again," she shared.

I made my way into the study, where Dad typically spends hours at the computer surfing the internet, watching movies, and playing games. He was sitting in his nightgown and house slippers, rocking back and forth in his chair, moaning in a haunting low-pitched rumble that sent chills through me. This wasn't an ulcer.

"Dad, what's wrong?" I asked.

He just kept moaning. I put my hand on his forehead. It was clammy and drenched in sweat. My mother returned with the milk.

"Let's give him some milk and see if it helps," she said.

I looked at my father rocking and moaning. I had never seen him looking this uncomfortable before.

"Milk isn't going to help. We're taking him to the ER. Dad, are you ok with us taking you to the Emergency Room?" I asked.

He nodded yes. For my father not to fight going to the ER, I knew the pain he was experiencing was excruciating to the point where he couldn't deny it any longer. I was helping him up from the chair when he decided to speak as he leaned on my shoulder.

"Son, let me go wash my face and brush my hair before we go." He muttered.

I looked at my mother in surprise. She shrugged her shoulders and I got a glimpse of what she faces with him every day as his wife. I held his hand as he shuffled to his bathroom. He gazed at himself in the mirror for a moment, splashed water on his face and pat dried it off with a towel. Then, he slowly, deliberately reached for a brush and ran it through his hair repeatedly until it was to his liking. He turned to me, suddenly impatient with the exasperated and concerned look on my face.

"I have to be presentable son." He announced.

My mother helped me put a coat over his robe, and we walked him to the car. We were planning to take him to a hospital in Albany where his gastrointestinal doctor practiced – a long 45-minute drive from where they lived. The roads were abandoned and narrow, with few street lights to guide the way. The three of us sat muted by our own personalized reactions to what was happening: Dad engulfed by his pain and thoughts of his own mortality. Mom constricted by her fear and prospect of losing her life partner. I was paralyzed by the possible reality of seeing my Superman falter, and having to be the strong one in this situation. Dad finally broke the silence between his slow, controlled breaths.

"Go to Ellis Hospital son. They know me there."

"Ellis Hospital" I thought to myself. Of course.

We got Dad to Ellis Hospital's ER, which was conspicuously empty for an early Sunday morning. He was promptly seen by one of the ER doctors who took his history, examined him, and ordered an EKG. He reviewed it and showed it to me. There were changes on it consistent with a heart attack. A nurse came by to draw his blood and start an IV. My father looked at the ER physician and me as his hearing aids couldn't pick up our conversation.

"You can tell me what's going on. Be honest with me," he pleaded.

I didn't have the energy or time to mince words with him.

"Dad, you may be having a heart attack."

He nodded his head in affirmation of what he already knew. While we waited on the lab results to return I looked at my mother, who stood against the wall on the side of his bed, forever stalwart in her support of her husband. Worried and trying not to show it, she held back tears and didn't speak a word. I shifted back to Dad, and in that moment of silence I could see the fear on his face. His empty gaze looked upward, past the chatty nurse who was more interested in talking about herself than his abdominal pain, and through the wall that kept him boxed in that room. It was a gaze of weary resignation, of a strong man insidiously being worn down by one major medical crisis too many.

The labs came back within an hour to provide confirmation of the blatantly obvious. Dad was diagnosed with an acute myocardial infarction, a heart attack, and was admitted to the hospital. As the medication kicked in, his stomach pain improved, and a cadre of doctors from varying disciplines paraded through to oversee his medical care. Each would speculate how extensive the blockages to his heart were. Most assumed that he had only one blood vessel blocked, and confidently declared that he could be quickly treated by opening up the blocked vessel using an umbrella or just medication as primary management. We all agreed and listened to them, hoping for the best. We were all wrong. They discovered that Dad actually had four blood vessels to his heart blocked, ranging in extent from 70-90%. He was going to need bypass surgery at 81.

Hospitals are funny places. Depending on where you are in the course of your life, how you view and experience them can be drastically different. As a child, I saw them as places of wonderment and discovery, ignorant of the day-to-day life and death happenings transpiring there. As a young physician-in-training, they merely represented residences of employment and slave labor – places where I spent more time than I did at home, and where I optimistically thought I could diagnose any illness and successfully treat any disease. As an adult patient, they were flawed houses of healing and rejuvenation, where I would be forced to relinquish any sense of control and trust to the nurturers who were charged with managing my health. As a caregiver for an ill and aging parent, I now saw them as potential deathtraps. Hospitals had morphed into institutions where incompetent nurses and equally incompetent doctors were hell-bent on not providing the best care my father could receive. As my perception of hospitals shifted to this final pessimistic train stop, my new role as patient family member was to do anything I could to make sure they didn't kill my father.

Dad's cardiac bypass surgery was scheduled for a Friday, two days after they had discovered the extent of his disease. But the moments leading up to the surgery didn't go quite as planned. I had returned to Philly to arrange time off so I could support my parents. The clinic was extremely supportive and granted me the time. I packed my things and tried to sleep that Wednesday night but couldn't. My plan was to drive to New York early Thursday morning and be there for the surgery on Friday. My mind couldn't turn itself off. Thinking of Dad alone in his hospital room again for the second time in two months with a life threatening illness was not conducive to curbing insomnia.

Standing on His Shoulders

My phone started ringing at 5 a.m. and woke me just as I had started to doze off. It was my mother, out of breath and rushing to get to her car. She had been called by the hospital because they were bumping up Dad's surgery to that morning, a full day earlier than previously scheduled. After they transferred him to the cardiac intensive care unit at 10 p.m. Wednesday night, he told the nurse he was having some mild indigestion and needed some milk. He didn't tell her that this was the same pain he had when he first had the heart attack, so she just brought him the milk and left him alone, as his vital signs were stable. But at 4 a.m. the pain must have been unbearable that even a stubborn Haitian surgeon could not deny it. He broke down and told the nurse that he was having the same abdominal pain as when he had his heart attack. This was all happening even with him being on medications and closely monitored. The staff sprang into action and performed a procedure called an "aortic balloon pump," a device inserted into the aorta that helps ease the stress on and increases oxygen delivery to the heart. They were whisking him to surgery within hours, because he couldn't wait a full day without risking further damage.

I raced back to upstate New York that morning while they were performing surgery on my father. A drive that is only four and a half hours seemed like a lifetime while my mind scanned everything that was transpiring and reminded me just how useless I was in this process. I arrived at the hospital and met Mom. The two of us sat in the visitor's lounge and patiently waited for his surgery to be complete. After six long hours, the cardiac surgeon met with us and told us Dad was transferred to the intensive care unit. It wasn't an easy surgery, complicated by my father's age and his other medical conditions, but they thought he was ok and had him ready so we could see him.

Despite all the nurses' preparatory explanations on what to expect with loved ones after cardiac surgery, walking in Dad's room was an experience for which I was ill-prepared. It was reminiscent to how he looked when he was readmitted to the neurologic intensive care unit after the extension of his stroke – only one hundred times worse. He was attached to countless tubes and IV lines, seemingly coming from or inserted into every orifice and blood vessel. He resembled an odd human marionette, helplessly manipulated and kept alive by some unseen force. The ventilator calmly hummed a methodical rhythm as his chest rose up and down in perfect sync with the machine's cadence. We walked in to see him briefly, held his swollen hands and reassured him as he slept that we were there. That's all we could do.

Dad was extubated and removed from the ventilator the next day. When my mother and I came to see him, he was disoriented from a potent mix of post-surgical delirium and the pain medication. He had been speaking French with the nursing staff and spouting some conspiracy theory stories – something he never would do normally. Michelle arrived with my niece and nephew, Skylar and Addison, that night. They came to his room while he was still somewhat delirious and on bed restriction. His grandchildren kissed and hugged their Papa as he held my sister's hand and tried to speak through a voice still raspy from the trauma of the breathing tube. Michelle reached into her bag, pulling out the bear Dad had bought for her when she was only one year old, and calmly placed it on his chest. The same bear purchased with the money Mom had saved so he could buy a good winter coat for himself. The same bear they placed in her crib as she slept peacefully. She had kept it all these years. The furry toy was intact, but tattered and worn, its once bright golden fur now matted and patchy in various spots. The distinctive roar it used to make was now a barely audible whimper that could only be elicited by an overly vigorous shake. Dad stared curiously at it, as if reconnecting with an old friend.

"Michelle this is yours – I bought this for you," he whispered.

My sister, who I rarely see cry, was visibly shaken seeing him like this.

"Dad, just hold on to this for good luck as you recover," she told him.

He squeezed the bear close to his chest and closed his eyes as tears streamed down his face.

The next several days were challenging, and while I was prepared for the physical strain cardiac surgery would have on Dad, I was less equipped to handle the emotional impact it would have on him. Every day represented a new and different journey for which none of us were adequately prepared. His mood oscillated from consummate depression pregnant with declarations to Mom that he was not afraid to die, to moments of laughter and playful banter about his Haitian resilience. But with every day, slowly and surely, we saw a progression in his physical and emotional state. One by one, the intrusive tubes and wires that sustained his life decreased in number. His chest pain was slowly diminishing and he was beginning to rise from the bed and chair to walk short distances down the hall with physical therapy.

As the physical advances declared their arrival, improvements in his emotional well-being accompanied them. His smile returned. His hearty laugh came back with renewed vigor. While exhausted and obviously disheartened by all that had transpired, he began to see a brightening of the dark cloud that had hung over him during this whole ordeal. Much like he had done while his condition improved after his stroke in 2000, Dad insisted on talking with whomever would come in his room as the days moved past his surgery. He had a steady stream of physician colleagues, friends, pulmonologists, cardiologists, nurses, physician assistants, phlebotomists, surgical techs, and other hospital staff who had worked with him during his glory days as a practicing surgeon. They would ask him how he was feeling physically. He would say he was "OK," then quickly change the subject to anything but his medical condition. How were their children doing? Had they collected any interesting watches recently? What cars were they considering purchasing? Again I found myself becoming increasingly aggravated with Dad's insistence on denial, and his guests' apparent lack of consideration about the seriousness of his condition.

As I sat seething with anger about a dynamic that had not changed in over a decade, suddenly I got it. Paying attention to the medical details of Dad's condition while he was in the hospital was *my* job, not his. In his older years, with his hearing gone and his medical acumen not quite as sharp from being retired for thirteen years, his super physician armor had slowly been eroding away. Underneath this shell was an 81-year-old man with multiple serious medical issues, exposed and vulnerable for all to see. It wasn't that my father didn't care about the minutia of his own medical condition. It wasn't that his visitors were maliciously overlooking the serious circumstances under which they were seeing him. Dad was actively coping with the challenging reality of aging in the best way he knew how – human connectedness. A warm smile, a gentle touch to the leg or hand, a kiss on the forehead, or an embrace from familiar arms were all gestures coming from the people he worked alongside, treated as patients, or enjoyed the journey of life with as friends. They helped him heal and challenged his spirit to remember he was alive. The dose of the blood thinner? The level of heart muscle enzymes in the blood? My mother and I were charged with keeping track of those pesky details while he focused on what was really helping him heal - the people surrounding him. They facilitated his adjustment to this transition more than any oral or intravenous medication ever could.

An interesting revelation also developed during Dad's hospital stay this time. For someone who spent the majority of his life telling me that there was only one race, the "human race" - he was now more sensitive and keenly focused on his status as a Black man than I had ever seen him before. The White Argentinean male nurse, whose lack of personal relation skills in dealing with my father infuriated him, was attributed to his "melanin" bias. The Black nurses' aide, who fanned herself and appeared to be revolted by the smell from my father losing control of his bladder, must have simply seen him as "just some old Black guy" whom she didn't respect due to her own self-hatred. The twenty-three-year-old Black male ICU technician studying to be a doctor while working full time, seemed very deferential and respected Dad as an elder Black statesman. The Ghanaian food server who waved at him and smiled every time he came to bring him a meal, he connected to him because they were both Black men.

My father absorbed all these hospital interactions after his surgery, particularly those he shared with other Black men. He experienced how each of these persons were witnessing not just an elderly Black male patient recovering from cardiac surgery, but a former Chief of Surgery at St. Clare's Hospital. He commented on how they looked at him and acknowledged all that he had done for the hospital and community in the past, and this made him proud. He hoped beyond hope that if the Black hospital staff saw the respect with which the other doctors and nurses treated him, they would be inspired to continue to strive to succeed in their own individual lives. After spending close to 50 years in the United States, maybe acknowledging diversity in the human race wasn't such a bad idea after all.

While Dad resided in the ICU those days following his surgery, I would stay a little bit longer after my mother, sister, niece, and nephew would venture on the thirty-minute drive back home. I liked to sit with him during those serene times, pretending we were simply discussing politics while watching birds at the lake or eating Roy Rogers chicken on a pit stop to Princeton. He would sit up in his cardiac chair, carelessly drifting in and out of consciousness while the nurses fluttered in and out of his room. This was a needed rest that had escaped him for the three months he suffered from the effects of the blood clot in his lungs and the blockages of the arteries to his heart. I would watch how his brow crinkles would relax, his lips part ever so slightly, and his breath become calm, as the rhythm of the heart monitors would serenade him to sleep. During one of these moments, as I was paying appreciative attention to how his chest rose and fell without interruption, he opened his eyes slowly and gazed over at me.

"Dave" he beckoned.

"Yeah Dad"

"You know, I have an idea for something I want you to patent."

I looked at him. Was he disoriented again? Unsure what he was talking about, I just decided to listen. He continued.

"You know, after surgery, you get very constipated. You can't go to the bathroom and it's very uncomfortable. And you don't know how humiliating it is to have these young pretty nurses reach inside you to help with your bowel movements."

"Go on…" I said.

"So instead of having a nurse manually reach inside you with her finger and pull the nuggets out, you could just get a small tube that has some lubrication, irrigate the area, use suction and suck the crap out of you. That would be great. You could make a lot of money off something like that."

"That sounds great Dad. What would you call it?"

He paused and looked at me slyly – a thinking man's physician to the very end.

"I would call it, 'The Pooper Scooper'."

He put his head back, closed his eyes and smiled ear to ear, content in his creative idea and still intact sense of humor. I kissed him on the forehead, left the hospital room and headed to my car. Things were going to be alright.

Epilogue

I go to the Caribbean for vacation at least once a year because, on a visceral level, it rejuvenates my spirit and replenishes my soul. Regardless of which island I visit, my favorite place is right on the beach, where I can admire majestic mountains in the distance and how they tower over the stark turquoise ocean. My last trip to St. Martin I sat in the sand at Orient Beach on the French side, peacefully monitoring the water's rhythmic movement. I was joined by a small black and golden spotted dog, who regally positioned itself on a dry pallet of fine sand and seaweed next to me. The gentle ocean breeze made its ears flop back as he closed his eyes to meet it, part from fatigue, part from the same innate pleasure every dog receives from the wind caressing its face from outside the window of a moving car. The pulsating waves of the ocean passionately licked the shore in a clockwork fashion, reminding me that my heart was still beating and I was alive. The sky was clear and endless, whispering eternity in my ear and suggesting the infinite possibilities of life. I took it all in and just tried to be present in the moment.

During these occasions when everything stops, I think about Dad. I embrace the beautiful accent of the islands and how life in the United States can be made rudely complicated by manufactured ruminations. He often speaks of his desire to return to this former Caribbean life he once knew, while I try to capture fleeting glimpses of this tranquil existence whenever and wherever I can. Visions of Morne L'Hopital appear when I close my eyes and I can hear Papa's feet over the leaves as he brought Dad to Tante Jeanne and Grand Dede so many years ago. I come here because it brings me home.

If you asked my father whether he envisioned seeing himself live to be over 80 years old, he would definitively tell you no, especially after his stroke in 2000. There were many times during his battle to survive when he thought he wouldn't make it through, and probably many more since. If you then ask him what kept him motivated to fight the adverse winds of aging and illness, he would likely tell you it was his family and the prospect of returning to his passion as a surgeon, in that order. When it comes to family, I know he cherishes the moments with my mother, sister and me during the holidays. But his main inspiration to live comes in the form of his two grandchildren, Skylar and Addison.

When they come to visit "Papa" and "Grandma" for holidays or vacations, just the anticipation of seeing them lifts his mood and makes his heart ascend to the heavens. When they actually arrive, regardless of how the piercing back pain or damaged hearing from the stroke is affecting him, Dad radiates with an energetic happiness that is rich and palpable. In them he sees a reimagining of Michelle and me. They are a version of us from a new generation, and he gets a second chance to be a father and positive influence again, to teach life lessons again, and to help guide them into adulthood as a wise elder should.

While connections with his immediate family have provided him nourishment over this past decade, the wear and tear of older age and not seeing close relatives from Haiti has taken its toll on his spirit. Dad has never been afraid of dying but now he repeatedly exclaims "don't ever get old son," as if I had a choice in the matter. People always say how young my father looks for his age. He does look youthful for an octogenarian, but appearances do not belie the passage of Father Time and how it can insidiously erode the daily internal human mechanics and routine functions we often take for granted.

For Dad, if there was a button he could press that could stop or completely reverse the aging process, he would do it in a heartbeat. His once intact hearing now requires bilateral aids so that he can carry on conversations and fully comprehend what people are saying. His previously well-lubricated and mobile joints stiffen frequently, causing him pain and difficulty with movement. His ankles, those that unwaveringly supported him while he effortlessly ambulated through hospital corridors, now fill up with fluid and require daily doses of water pills to keep the swelling down. His back, the once sturdy foundation of bone, sinewy muscle and nerves that held him upright while he repaired thousands of human bodies, is now riddled with painful inflammation that makes it difficult to walk. The stroke now manifests in intermittent disturbances in balance, temperature and pain recognition on his left side. The more recent bouts with the pulmonary embolus and heart attack now necessitate oxygen administration at night and cut short his exercise capabilities. These are all difficult reminders of exactly how fragile the human body becomes with the inevitable passage of time.

Despite all this, what has been truly amazing to witness is my father's indomitable spirit and resilience. While it would be easy to simply attribute this to his Haitian roots, perhaps the most important component of this resilience is my mother, who has been alongside him during his journey for almost five decades. She is the most authentic example of unconditional love that I have seen in my life. Today, they are partners when selling antiques online. He takes the pictures and does the write ups; she posts them on Ebay and handles the sales, packaging, and communication with customers. Dad does daily exercises to get his back and joints warmed up, and she is there carefully monitoring him with every movement. Mom makes sure he takes his daily medications and vitamins, which he surely would not take if she weren't there to remind him. She brings him to all of his doctor's appointments and schedules his calendar so he attends his follow-up visits. While he spends hours on the computer listening to traditional Haitian Meringue, Compas, and Classical music, reading about current surgical knowledge and techniques, watching movies on Netflix, or socializing on Facebook, she sits and watches television in the adjacent room, understanding his need for that time to himself. She faithfully prepares every meal for him and remains flexible keeping up with a heart healthy diet. She even handles his mood swings with the dexterity of a seasoned therapist. Don't be fooled for a moment, Dad is certainly a strong Haitian man - but he is a stronger Haitian man because of the Ukrainian woman who stands by his side.

I have gone through many changes with my father over the years, and it has truly been a journey of ever-evolving experiences and perceptions. When I was a child, he was the invincible, all-knowing Superman who could do nothing wrong. During my youth and teenage years, he became my biggest adversary, my stiffest competition and, oftentimes, the bane of my existence. As a young adult, I grew to appreciate his wisdom and knowledge, reluctantly starting to digest some of the life lessons he was so desperately trying to teach me as a child. Through my transition from young adulthood to full adulthood, I saw him as the single largest human influence in my life and the man whom I aspired to be more like - perfectly imperfect. I now consider him one of my best friends, and the individual whose opinion matters the most to me. Our relationship has been a flawed, awkward, and beautiful dance. It is a dance that cannot be rehearsed or scripted, but merely gets more polished and refined as time goes on. We have stepped on each other's toes, missed a beat here and there, and at times fallen down completely. Yet he is the reason why I continue to dance, persist to rise up when I fall, and continue to stand on his shoulders to see further than he has during his lifetime.

The moments when I've learned the most from Dad were not those when we got along famously, but when we butted heads the hardest. Some may say that this is a consequence of our similar genetic makeup, and maybe this is true. What I have realized, however, is that the greatest lessons on human behavior occur during periods of struggle and conflict. Frederick Douglass once said, "Without struggle, there is no progress" to describe the conflict in overturning slavery and obtaining equal human and civil rights as Black people in the United States. Although we currently have a Black male president in Barack Obama, this quote still rings true with regards to larger battles against the persistent scourge of social injustices and racial inequality in the United States. But perhaps for us as Black men, it is a much more appropriate quote that describes the essence of how we interact with each other and ourselves. One truth is certain when it comes to Dad – he was always there. Perhaps not always physically or in the exact way in which I desired him to be present, but he was there. This is the man who would patiently wait on me as a child while I would chase ants on the sidewalk while walking to the hospital with him. He's the one who threw me on his back and ran me into the house while the wasps from a nest I had disturbed stung him unmercifully. I couldn't always appreciate everything he did for me growing up despite watching him work endless surgical cases to provide for his family. I can see clearly now. I am truly thankful for his watchful eye monitoring every step I have ventured to take into adulthood.

Standing on His Shoulders

Dad is not the same person he was when I was five years old, and I certainly am not the same person I was back then, or even when I was twenty or thirty years of age. The beauty of life and human beings is that we are not static entities, frozen in time and space, destined to be the same, act the same, and feel the same for the rest of our lives. Our interactions with people and life experiences change us in subtle and not-so-subtle ways every day. Without some of the struggles I have had with my father, I would not have matured and learned half the life lessons I have. I realized my academic potential because of him. I appreciate how I am uniquely positioned as a Black man in this society because of him. I came into my own sense of manhood because of him. I understand, appreciate, and embrace my romantic attractions to men because of him. I am a better physician and healer because of him. Perhaps most importantly, the good times and struggles with my father have taught me a great deal about the naïve young boy I once was, and the kind of man who I continually strive to be.

Today, when I make the trek to wintry upstate New York as a man in my mid-forties and I see my Dad, it's not with the same expectations or pursuit of activities which predominated our interactions when we were both younger. We don't go to the park to run around and fly kites in an overcast sky. We don't venture in the backyard to throw a football or kick a soccer ball around until our legs are good and sore. We don't plan expensive trips to faraway places that would require countless hours on planes, trains, and automobiles. We don't stay up until the wee hours of the morning watching sports, screaming at the television as if the New York Knicks or Yankees players can hear our impassioned pleas.

Instead, we take a trip to the local theater to catch the latest Denzel Washington film with my mother. We sit at a small kitchen table in the mornings, discussing politics and current events while watching the infinite species of birds with Mom as she prepares a breakfast fit for kings. We sit side-by-side and watch a football or basketball game on a lazy Sunday afternoon. We watch a Netflix movie on his computer, where the stereo speakers are loud enough that he can hear clearly. We drive together, not to Princeton, but through the snow-covered landscape of upstate New York back roads to run small errands. During these times we are together, when the air is still and the moments are small, my father talks to me and imparts knowledge as he has done for decades. I listen. His voice hums with the abundance of the African Diaspora and the resilience of an independent Black republic. I listen. The sound coming from his lips is a glorious and well-orchestrated symphony of history and memories, brimming with overlapping feelings of contentedness and regret, fulfilled expectations, and dreams deferred. I listen, knowing that these are snapshots in time I wish we had experienced together much sooner in our lives. I listen, understanding fully that these are occasions I wish would never end, but I know ultimately will.

I listen, and watch him walk on water all over again.

About the Author

D avid J Malebranche was born and raised in Schenectady, New York, and is a board-certified Internal Medicine physician. He received a M.D. from Emory University and a master's degree from the Mailman School of Public Health at Columbia University. He is a clinical and research expert in the fields of sexual health, LGBT health, and racial disparities in HIV prevention and treatment. He currently lives in Atlanta, Georgia.

Made in the USA
Columbia, SC
15 June 2022